# Private Practice:

A Survival Guide for Mental Health Practioners Entering Private Practice

By:
Angela Mohan
Association for Advanced Training
in the Behavioral Sciences

For my parents,
Jim Mohan and Florence Perez LaManno,
without whom I wouldn't be who and where I am today

And for my husband Larry,
dearest friend, companion, and love of my life—

# Private Practice:

## A (survival) Guide for Mental Health Practioners Entering Private Practice

### TABLE OF CONTENTS

**CHAPTER 1: INTRODUCTION** .................. 1

**CHAPTER 2: WHO ARE YOU?** ................ 9
   Your vision of yourself ......................... 9
   Theoretical orientation ....................... 14
   To be or not to be a private practitioner? ......... 15
   Money options in the meantime ................ 15
   What kind of clients do you want? .............. 18
   Fee setting .................................. 22
   Pager availability ............................. 25
   Phone availability ............................ 27
   Fee for phone sessions ........................ 28
   No-show policy/late cancellations/24-hour cancellation requirements ..................... 29

**CHAPTER 3: OFFICE SPACE AND START UP EXPENSES** ..................................... 35
   Sharing an office ............................. 35
      Phones .................................. 37
      Scheduling - on an office master or set days and times? ............................... 38
      Renting by the hour ...................... 40
   Having your own office ........................ 43

# Table of Contents

- Safety issues .................................... 44
- Your waiting room ............................... 45
- Your physical office space ....................... 47
- Isolation ........................................ 49
- Tenant improvements (e.g., carpet, paint) ......... 49
- Leasing vs. renting .............................. 49
- Cleaning crew/arrangements ....................... 50
- Water/electricity/air conditioning/heat ........... 51
- Start-up expenses ................................... 51
  - Office space - per/hour or first and last ....... 51
  - Furniture ....................................... 52
  - Business cards .................................. 53
  - Calendar/palm pilot ............................. 54
  - Business stationary/letterhead .................. 55
  - Office "incidentals" ............................ 55

## CHAPTER 4: EQUIPMENT/FURNITURE ............ 59

- Equipment ........................................... 59
  - Telephones and answering machines/voicemail ..... 59
  - Fax machines .................................... 61
  - Pagers .......................................... 61
  - Computer ........................................ 63
  - Locking filing cabinet .......................... 64
  - Door plaque/name in building directory .......... 64
  - Palm Pilot vs. pen and paper .................... 65
- Furniture ........................................... 66
  - Couches vs. chairs .............................. 66
  - Ergonomic/special chairs ........................ 67
  - Lamps-floor and table ........................... 68
  - Coffee and end tables and waiting room furniture ... 68
  - Music system .................................... 68
  - Magazines ....................................... 69

| | |
|---|---|
| Desk | 70 |
| Bookshelves | 70 |
| Prints/decorations | 70 |
| **CHAPTER 5: FORMS** | **73** |
| Intake form/client information sheet | 73 |
| Confidentiality | 74 |
| Consent for treatment/treatment of a minor | 74 |
| Office policy form | 75 |
| Release of confidential information | 75 |
| Assignment of insurance benefits | 77 |
| Termination/discharge letter | 78 |
| "What is therapy?"/informed consent | 78 |
| Initial assessment forms | 79 |
| Mental Status Examination | 80 |
| Personal history forms | 80 |
| Treatment form | 81 |
| Session/progress notes | 81 |
| Crisis information sheet | 86 |
| No harm contract/no suicide contract | 87 |
| Discharge summary | 88 |
| Billing sheet (regular) | 89 |
| **CHAPTER 6: GETTING BUSINESS FOR YOUR BUSINESS** | **93** |
| Advertising | 93 |
| Newspapers | 96 |
| Flyers | 97 |
| MD's/psychiatrists | 97 |
| Trade magazines (e.g., parenting classes in a parenting magazine) | 97 |
| Mailings and professional newsletters | 98 |
| Internet/web-sites | 98 |
| Posting at local coffeehouses etc. | 99 |

## Table of Contents — Private Practice

- Phone books ... 99
- Referral sources ... 100
  - Personal ... 100
  - Other therapists and medical professionals ... 100
  - Giving seminars and/or educational classes ... 100
  - Networking, networking, networking! ... 101
  - Interviewing the masters ... 103
  - Getting the word out about what you do ... 104
- Being a provider ... 105
  - Medi-cal ... 105
  - Employee Assistance Programs ... 105
  - Victims of crime ... 106
  - Managed care provider panel ... 107

### CHAPTER 7: MONEY MATTERS ... 111
- Money - payment up front or bill insurance and take the co-pay? ... 112
- Quarterly taxes, Social Security and Medicare ... 113
- Retirement accounts ... 115
- Time-off, scheduling it in to your practice ... 117
- Taxes ... 119
- Billing ... 121
  - HCFA 1500 form ... 121
  - Billing software ... 122
  - Individual insurance claim forms ... 123
  - Collecting overdue money ... 124
  - Business checking account ... 126
  - Business credit card ... 126

### CHAPTER 8: SELF CARE ... 129
- Avoiding therapist burnout ... 129
- Getting support ... 130
- Affirmations/inspirations ... 131

## Table of Contents

    Anthony Robbins/Dale Carnegie/Dr. Phil . . . . . . . . . 132
    Audio tapes/books/movies . . . . . . . . . . . . . . . . . . . 132
    Journaling . . . . . . . . . . . . . . . . . . . . . . . . . . . . . . . 133
    Be your best therapist . . . . . . . . . . . . . . . . . . . . . . 133
    Visualizations. . . . . . . . . . . . . . . . . . . . . . . . . . . . . 134
    Scheduling in breaks for yourself (including vacations and sick time) . . . . . . . . . . . . . . . . . . . . 135
    Exercise . . . . . . . . . . . . . . . . . . . . . . . . . . . . . . . . . 137
    Your own therapy/support group . . . . . . . . . . . . . . 137
    Taking professional enhancement seminars/continuing education . . . . . . . . . . . . . . . 138
    Going on retreat. . . . . . . . . . . . . . . . . . . . . . . . . . . 139
    Massages/facials/the pampering world . . . . . . . . . . 139

**CHAPTER 9: MISCELLANEOUS. . . . . . . . . . . . . . . 143**
    Sole proprietorship vs. partnership vs. incorporated . . . . . . . . . . . . . . . . . . . . . . . . . . . . . 143
    Fictitious business names, a.k.a., "doing business as" statement . . . . . . . . . . . . . . . . . . . . . 145
    Referring to a medical professional . . . . . . . . . . . . 146
    Referring to another mental health professional . . . 147
    Insurance issues . . . . . . . . . . . . . . . . . . . . . . . . . . 149
    Legal issues/legal consultation . . . . . . . . . . . . . . . . 151
    Licensing issues . . . . . . . . . . . . . . . . . . . . . . . . . . . 151
    City business license . . . . . . . . . . . . . . . . . . . . . . . 152
    Continuing education . . . . . . . . . . . . . . . . . . . . . . . 152
    Diagnostic and Statistical Manual of Mental Disorders . . . . . . . . . . . . . . . . . . . . . . . . . . . . . . . 153
    Code procedure book (CPT) . . . . . . . . . . . . . . . . . . 154
    Business files . . . . . . . . . . . . . . . . . . . . . . . . . . . . . 154

# CHAPTER 1: INTRODUCTION

Welcome. What a thrill that you picked up this book and are on your way to joining the ranks of private practice therapists. GOOD FOR YOU!

Since you have chosen this book, I can assume that you are a mental health professional. This manual is geared to address the needs of Marriage and Family Therapists, Licensed Clinical Social Workers, Psychologists, and Licensed Professional Counselors.

My experience has been that, regardless of the education, training, and experience you have received as a mental health professional, you have been unable to find the necessary and relevant information in the field regarding the practicalities of starting your own business as a private practice professional.

To this end, I have attempted to fill this need. Here then is your very own survival guide to entering private practice. My hope is that the information provided here will assist you in transitioning into a fulfilling private practice.

This book is meant to serve as a GUIDE or a RESOURCE. It is <u>not</u> meant to bog you down with information you already know, nor is it intended to serve merely as a "how to" book about getting your private practice up and running. Rather, it is designed to ACTIVATE the resources that you already possess, and to provide you with resources you have not yet come across.

I have attempted to include the information a mental health professional would need who has NOT previously set up his/her own private practice and who may or may not be well versed in the business of setting up and running a small business. It is NOT intended to be a comprehensive "list" of things to do in order to make that happen. Rather, it has been set up as a handbook of information and options. As you go through this book, I trust that you will note the places that appeal to you as a mental health practitioner, and apply yourself to those areas accordingly.

I have a number of beliefs that drove me when I was writing this book.

- I believe that mental health practitioners are among the most flexible and bright professionals on the planet. (I am, admittedly, a tad biased, but there you have it)

- I believe that we chose a profession that encourages us to learn new things every day, and to grow personally and professionally every time a client walks through our doors. I believe that this learning and desire for growth characterizes our profession.

- I believe that our chosen profession can be an isolative one. That being said, we could probably use some assistance with collaboration and the distribution of information, especially when we are new to the BUSINESS of doing therapy.

- I believe that, once the logistics of private practice are enumerated clearly and concisely, each of you will be able to set up your private practice in a way that best suits YOU. There is no "right" or "best" way to set up your private practice, just as there is no template for what *constitutes* a private practice. Once you have options available to you, you will be able to make the choices that make the most sense to you as a professional.

- I believe that, if only each of us had a group of already established professionals helping us set up our private practices, this process wouldn't seem so overwhelming.

- And last, but certainly not least, I believe that all tasks become incredibly "do-able" if you CHUNK THEM DOWN into bite sized pieces. Most tasks, which can feel overwhelming and enormous when taken as a whole, will seem very manageable when taken in small bite sized pieces.

And so, this is what I have attempted to do with this handbook. This is your "professional support group"; acknowledging the joys and pitfalls of the business, sharing the nuts-and-bolts information of setting up your business, and offering advice in getting over the inevitable hurtles facing you during this transition.

So, play with this guidebook. Flip through the pages, do the chapters in whatever order you want. Whatever you do, **MAKE IT YOUR OWN**. Do not read through this book as just another piece of interesting literature about being a therapist in our ever-changing professional world. Do the exercises. Fill in the blanks. Finish the stem sentences. Play around. This is your life and your time. Make it work the way YOU want it to work.

# Chapter 1    Private Practice

You'll find an inordinate number of questions in this book. One of my beliefs is that YOU AND ONLY YOU can determine how you want to set up your private practice. There is no right way to do it. For those of us who like to couch things in therapeutic language there isn't even a "better" or "more effective" way to do it. There is simply YOUR way. To that end, the questions are there to assist you in generating your own answers so that, when you get to the end of this book, you will be clearer about your practice and how you would like it set up and run.

One of the best ways to do that is to ask yourself, "What do I want from reading this book?" the answer to this may give you a good starting idea of where you want to be headed next in your professional life. Let's take it one step at a time.

I picked up this book because:

- ☐ I want some good ideas about how to get started in setting up a private practice
- ☐ I'd like to hear how other therapists' set up their practices
- ☐ I want to know where to begin
- ☐ I'd like to expand my resources about my business
- ☐ I don't want to have to "recreate the wheel" in setting up my practice, I want to hear how other people have done it
- ☐ I already have a private practice but I want to expand it from part-time to full-time work
- ☐ I'm unhappy at the clinic where I'm currently working and I'd like to start branching out on my own
- ☐ I'm in a group practice and I want my own office
- ☐ I have a practice but I want to expand/revamp it

Private Practice                                                Chapter 1

- ☐ I'm feeling "stuck" professionally and I want some new ideas

- ☐ I see most of my clients on a cash basis. I would like to know how to get signed up to be on insurance panels

- ☐ My internship is allowing me to take my clients with me when I get my own office, but I'm a little nervous about making the move. I'd like some encouragement while I transition out of my clinic/counseling center.

- ☐ I'm afraid if I start a private practice I won't see other therapists very often. I think I'll burn out if I'm doing this work all by myself. I want to know how to avoid this.

- ☐ Fill in your own answer

_____

_____

_____

Speaking of which, how about figuring out what you would like to **GET** out of this book before going any farther? Check all the boxes that apply.

- ☐ Get great ideas for my practice.

- ☐ Well, I HAVE been thinking about starting my own practice; maybe this book will have some ideas for me.

- ☐ I just feel lost and overwhelmed when I even THINK about starting my own business. Where do I go? What do I need to do? HELP!

- ☐ Well, even though I'm still only half way through my hours, I want to know what's going to be ahead of me when the time comes.

© Association For Advanced Training

# Chapter 1 — Private Practice

- ☐ I feel overwhelmed when I start to think about starting my own practice. What if I'm not good enough? When if I fail? Have other therapists' felt this way?
- ☐ I want to be out on my own already! Enough with working for someone else.
- ☐ I don't need this information. I already have my MBA/I've worked in the business community all of my life. But what if having a therapy private practice is different business-wise from being a CPA? I'd better get it just in case.
- ☐ I want to know what information I need to get going. I don't even know what questions to ask at this point.
- ☐ I want to know WHAT I DON'T KNOW. I want to be able to ask the better questions that will help me to get mobilized in my private practice.

So, the sky's the limit for you. Play with this book and information in it. Find what works for you. Explore some new options. And most of all HAVE A GOOD TIME.

To that end, may I recommend that you give yourself permission to write all over this book? Now I know that that suggestion goes against one of our most deeply held beliefs about the defacement of books, (and what will happen to you if you should, heaven forbid, actually WRITE in one), but this is meant to be essentially a WORKBOOK for your private practice. You'll get lots more out of this book if you do the exercises, make notes in the margins, and highlight the sections you want to remember.

**NOTES**

## CHAPTER 2: WHO ARE YOU?

Each one of us, whether we are mental health professionals, accountants, or lawyers, must have a vision of what we are about in our practice. We must know where we are going and how, in general, we plan to get there. WHY? Because the brain is activated by goals, and without them, we run the risk of becoming a proverbial ship without a rudder. Does this mean that you have to be LOCKED INTO your initial vision of yourself and your practice? Of course not. So many therapists are afraid of being pigeonholed, or of cutting off the possibilities of seeing a particular kind of client because they have identified themselves in a specific way. That couldn't be farther from the truth.

### Your vision of yourself

A vision statement addresses the MOST BASIC parts of who you are as a therapist. It talks about what you believe, about the kind of work you do in your practice, and about the ways in which you believe that people grow and change in their worlds and in their lives.

Creating a vision of ourselves and of our businesses actually helps us to be clearer about what services we provide. That in turn enables us to provide a higher level of services to our clients and customers.

Have an answer ready when someone calls your office and asks you what you do. What do you believe causes people to change?

Remember that the "public" doesn't know what we do; some (or much) of this will be an issue of educating the consumers. And the more knowledgeable our clients are about what therapy entails and what they can expect in treatment, the better clients they will be and the better able you will be to serve their needs.

So, check all that apply. This will be a good starting place for you to begin developing a "vision statement" about yourself and your business.

- ☐ I believe people get "stuck" when they don't have the information they need to make those changes. Change occurs when they are provided with EDUCATION and INFORMATION to make those changes. Therapists facilitate the acquisition of that knowledge.

- ☐ People need to be HEARD. Once that happens, and you can reflect back to them what they've said, they can begin to make changes in their lives.

- ☐ Insight is the best way to get to client change. Once someone UNDERSTANDS why they have been behaving a certain way, then they can make new choices about how to behave differently.

- ☐ I can assist my clients in improving the quality of their lives, through hooking them up with community resources and providing them with the support they will need to access those resources.

- ☐ If I can help my clients make BEHAVIORAL changes in his/her life, then the rest will follow. Once they are behaving differently in their lives, they will begin to FEEL better about themselves and THINK DIFFERENTLY about their circumstances. This will enable them to make more effective and lasting changes in their lives and in their relationships.

- ☐ If I can help broaden the knowledge of human behavior for individuals and society, I will help improve the conditions of both.

- ☐ If you simply provide a nurturing environment, and have UNCONDITIONAL POSITIVE REGARD for your clients, they will make the changes that best fit them in their lives. People are to be trusted with their own lives and their own process of change.

- ☐ Once you have completed the necessary psychological testing of an individual, you will be able to intervene in meaningful ways to help that individual improve the conditions of his/her life.

- ☐ Once people understand the MULTIGENERATIONAL TRANSMISSION PROCESS and how it impacts their life currently, they will be able to make greater moves toward DIFFERENTIATION with their families and with their significant others.

Okay? Okay. I think you get the idea. All of us, whether we've ever really looked deeply into the subject or not, have VERY SPECIFIC ideas about what makes psychotherapy work. We have deeply held beliefs that drive us in our clinical work, and it's a good idea to find out what those beliefs are so that we can both capitalize on them and also beware (Be aware) of them, because all theoretical beliefs have shortcomings. If you don't know yours, it will likely blindside you one of these days, when you least expect it. (Of course, why would it be

## Chapter 2 — Private Practice

when we were expecting it? Much more fun to be completely baffled for a while and then have a nice "ah-ha", don't you think?)

It's best to have a solid idea of who you are as a clinician and how your beliefs about therapy help determine the kinds of clients you see and the work you do. It also helps us avoid inadvertently seeing clients whom we have little affinity for and who also perhaps have little to no affinity for the work that we do. For example, think about this scenario:

> *An angry, rebellious teenager is brought in by his parents. His school counselor states he has been getting into a lot of fights lately and is about to suspend him. Oh, and by the way, he's also using drugs. A lot of them.*

Let's say you primarily do insight-oriented therapy and work towards the goal of understanding the patterns of relationships. You also mostly work with co-dependency issues and a good part of your practice is made up of middle-aged women. You talk to your clients about self-care, nurturing days, and their inner child. Your office space is quiet, with fountains babbling in the background and Mozart on the stereo. Oh, yeah, and teenagers, (boys especially) make you nervous.

Think you'll be tremendously effective in treating this teenager? Probably not. Your strengths lie elsewhere, and failing to acknowledge that can be frustrating to you and pointless to our angry teenager who needs some clear structure and behavior modification before he lands in juvenile hall.

So, identify your beliefs about therapy and focus on the kinds of clients that will BENEFIT from working with you and who "buy" your brand of therapy. We all have specific populations who will benefit from working with us and populations who won't. Find out which is which for you.

## DON'T TRY TO BE ALL THINGS TO ALL PEOPLE

Along this same vein, I once asked a therapist to describe her practice to me. She said, "I see individuals, couples, children and teenagers. I do groups with women, men, divorce issues, parenting and anger management. I work in the framework of life transitions, mood disorders, addictions, and family of origin work. I take a developmental, family systems, cognitive behavioral approach in my work."

As a consumer, (and remember that that's who we serve, **consumers**), wouldn't that answer stupefy you? Wouldn't you be _more_ confused after hearing that than when you started? If we want to start de-mystifying the therapeutic process, (and we'd better do it soon before people lose <u>all</u> patience with us), we have to start giving our client/consumers straight answers.

I am by no means recommending that each of us has to have specialization's and that those must define who we are as therapists and how we do the business and work of therapy. But somewhere along the road, there are just some clients that each of us will work better with than other clients.

The fact is, no matter how outspoken we are about whom we do or don't see, (or, to put it into more therapeutic parlance, whom we _prefer_ to see or not see) each of us makes choices about the kinds of clients that we like to work with. We don't always have a choice about who shows up on our doorsteps that first session, but we CERTAINLY have a choice thereafter.

And here's the deal on this topic, (and then I promise I'll move on to something more interesting), <u>there is absolutely</u>

nothing wrong with preferring to see certain types of clients. Again, capitalize on your strengths, go with what works for you as a clinician. Then you'll be able to create the kind of private practice that drives your forward and creates a lasting and satisfying business for yourself.

And again, DON'T TRY TO BE ALL THINGS TO ALL PEOPLE.

## Theoretical orientation

I think this has as much to do with the kind of practice we want to have as the kind of clients we choose. The issue is who you are currently and who you choose to be as a therapist. Basically, what I'm asking for here is, what are your orienting beliefs about therapy? To what school of thought do you affiliate yourself as a therapist? Are you fundamentally a psychodynamic therapist? Tend more towards Structural or Communications Theory? Social psychology? How about Extended Family Systems Theory? Cognitive-Behavioral? Social Behavioralism? Neurolinguistic programming? Hypnotherapy? Psychoneuroimmunology?

Chances are, if you have picked up this book, you know what these terms mean, but if you are John Q. Public, many of these terms would have little meaning. Find a way to describe to clients what it is that you do, in straightforward layman's terms.

Each of us has perhaps affiliated ourselves more or less with a particular orientation or school of thought, and then we "pull" interventions from various places to meet the needs of our clients. Identify your orienting thoughts and begin to conceptualize and articulate your general goals of therapy.

Have a "blurb" ready when someone calls you for the first time. Sure maybe all they're going to want to do initially is vent and have someone to listen to them, but it will be a better fit therapeutically in the long-run if you discuss this at the onset.

If you don't affiliate yourself with a particular school of thought, then describe what you strive for. What would mean "success" for you therapeutically?

## To be or not to be a private practitioner?

And now to the subject of doing what you do in a private practice setting rather than in a clinic or counseling center setting.

When you think of becoming a private practitioner, what most immediately comes to mind? If you're like most of us, it is a question that raises a great deal of anxiety and/or ambivalence.

Having a private practice is:

- ☐ An exciting thought
- ☐ A joy
- ☐ A virtual nightmare

When I think about being on my own, I:

- ☐ Can't wait
- ☐ Can't stop feeling nauseated
- ☐ Can't wait to stop feeling nauseated

## Money options in the meantime

While many of us think and feel that this is the best way to go, many others want or need or would like the security of a "steady" job, you know, one that pays you every couple of

# Chapter 2 — Private Practice

weeks and ensures that you won't, (in the immediate future at least), return to your "Top Ramen, Macaroni and Cheese" college days. To that end, there are NUMEROUS opportunities for employment, both full and part time, for the newly licensed professional. The following is a partial list, and is designed not so much as a comprehensive list as a "get the wheels turning" list. Here goes:

- ☐ <u>Counseling centers</u>: Many communities and cities have counseling centers that are anxious to employ licensed professionals. In general these agencies charge their clients on a sliding scale and they pay their mental health professionals a percentage of the charged fee. The percentage splits can range from 50/50 mental health professionals/counseling center to 70/30 or even 80/20. While this might not sound like a lot of money, it can provide the necessary base while you branch out. For example, on an $85/session client, you might get 50% ($42.50), 70% ($59.50) or 80% ($68.00). In addition, the counseling center generates its own referrals. The good news is that it that this frees up some of your energy and you don't have to generate your own referrals. The bad news is, *then you don't have to generate your own referrals*. You can quickly get out of practice (or never learn the skill at all) if you leave this key component up to someone else for too long.

- ☐ <u>County and state organizations</u>: Good heavens, none of us need to be told that there are ALWAYS opportunities with the various local government agencies. Heck, some of us cut our eyeteeth on them while we were racking up those necessary hours, and these government agencies are sometimes the reason we want SO BADLY to be out on our own. But before you dismiss county or government work out of hand, remember that these kinds of organizations can provide valuable commodities that are extremely appealing: stability, health insurance, security, and a steady paycheck. There's nothing wrong with getting a bit out of debt/back on your feet before launching the next wave on the world. These organizations are a great way of gaining valuable experience while still having a steady paycheck.

- ☐ <u>Foster Family Agency's and/or Group Homes</u>: Many county or state run organizations that deal with child abuse and neglect have several placement options for the children in their care; foster homes, foster family agencies, group homes and governmentally run institutions. The children in regular foster care are able to access mental health through the local Mental Health Organization listed in your area. The government run institutions, including shelter care placements and orphanages) generally have their own mental health professionals on staff. However, foster family agencies and Group homes frequently employ individual mental health professionals to provide the necessary services for their children.

- ☐ <u>Teaching, community colleges, adult education organizations, seminars, speeches</u>: These are great niches for mental health professionals because they so nicely dovetail into work in the counseling profession.

- ☐ <u>Coaching</u>: Professional coaching is the next (or at least the newest) wave of the future. There's lots of information out there, lots of seminars and classes and possibilities. I would refer you to the book *The New Private Practice* by Lynn Grodski for some clarifications about the differences between professional coaching and professional therapy. Also visit the Internet for the organizations that provide certification classes in coaching.

☐ **Hospitals, psychiatric or otherwise**: Many hospitals employ mental health professionals in a number of capacities. They can be case managers, therapists, crisis team members, group leaders, or social workers. Work in a hospital setting may depend on your license type, but it is nevertheless an excellent and oft times overlooked employment possibility.

So, those are some of the "bread and butter" employment opportunities. In the transition phase of becoming fully established in your full-time private practice, some support the bread and butter theory while others go for the "burn all bridges/avenues of escape" philosophy. For yourself, you must certainly take into account all of the financial variables that make up your world. You may have endless options because it is perfectly fine for you to go back to your "starving college" days. Or, you may have financial responsibilities that dictate that you move more slowing towards a full-time private practice. Either way, do what works best FOR YOU.

## What kind of clients do you want?

Who are you and/or who do you want to be as a practitioner? This is a particularly important question. Remember again, the "whys" come before the "hows." Think of what you want to do as a therapist: is it to change people's perceptions of themselves? Assist families in transitioning? Assist clients in accessing community resources? Become an expert at the assessment and treatment of personality disorders? Assist community organizations in meeting the needs of a diverse population? Enable couples to communicate effectively? Really think about this issue, because, in large part, it is what drives you daily (or at least what WILL drive you).

# Private Practice    Chapter 2

All of us have had to do thousands of pre-licensure hours in order to qualify to sit for our licensing exams. Internships come in a variety of packages and you may have found that you spent your time working with a fairly exclusive population of clients, or that you had a variety of client experiences. As a result of your internship time, you may have come away with what you would like to continue in your private practice. On the other hand, you may not have ever had the opportunity to experience what it was to work with an entire family, or with a particular population. Read through the following list with an eye to what strikes you as **fitting you** at this moment, even if you may not have necessarily had those experiences previously.

- ☐ Individuals – Do you enjoy seeing individuals as opposed to couples or families? Do you find that your style of therapy lends itself well to individuals? Did you primarily see individuals during your internship? Was that by choice or by conscription? Remember, individuals are the most common clients to show up on our doorsteps, but that doesn't mean that's the client base that you have to choose. Remember too that this is just to jog your brain to identify certain areas of *preference*; most practices are a combination of all kinds of clients.

- ☐ Couples – Like the communication stuff between couples? Love the dynamics and the movement of having a conflicted couple sitting in front of you trying to hash things out? Or do you find it overwhelming and discouraging? Couple's therapists pretty much know why see couples; they LOVE the dynamics, the tension, the ultimate resolve and the coming together of a couple.

- ☐ Families – Again, you've got to like the family movement and dynamics to like working with families and their various subsystems. If organized chaos doesn't unduly upset you, then families may be one of your areas. Also, many newly licensed therapists have never had the opportunity to work with a family system, so don't discard this out of hand just because it may sound intimidating. Family work can be tremendously exciting and rewarding.

☐ Groups – Some therapists are just naturally adept at running and managing groups and their dynamics. They find the variety of people exciting and challenging and the work rewarding. Many therapists also frequently start off by doing a group with another therapist, and work in a co-therapist situation. (Some therapist ONLY work in a co-therapist situation, believing that each therapist will balance out the other and enable them both to work more effectively with their clients)

☐ Children – Again, yes for some people, a resounding NO for others. And think too, what age group? Small children? School aged? Teenagers? (Stop groaning and saying "no way": teenagers are a GREAT population to work with - they just get a little bad publicity occasionally) Also, if you choose to work with children, think ahead to the issues involved in the additional space/equipment needed for this. (i.e. playrooms, sand trays, therapeutic games etc.)

☐ Specialty populations – Some therapists find themselves drawn to a particular group of people or particular issues: Domestic violence, Adults Molested as Children, Alanon, Victims of Crimes, Blended and Stepfamilies. Your practice can also have specialty sub-sets; perhaps you primarily see individuals but also run two Divorce Support Groups a week.

- ☐ <u>School, court or other psychological assessments</u> – Many mental health professionals like to focus on the area of assessment, and provide services individuals within the context of a variety of organizations and systems that benefit from those assessments.

This is only a short list/discussion of the various options available to you, the mental health professional. To further assist you in clarifying your professional goals regarding clients, check the boxes that apply in terms of who you see/who you would LIKE to see in your practice and what areas interest you professionally.

- ☐ Individuals
- ☐ Couples
- ☐ Families
- ☐ Groups
- ☐ Small children
- ☐ Teenagers
- ☐ The elder population
- ☐ Crisis/trauma victims
- ☐ Children in school settings
- ☐ Work with other mental health professionals
- ☐ Adults Molested as Children
- ☐ Alcoholics
- ☐ Professional consultation
- ☐ Public speaking
- ☐ Research
- ☐ Writing
- ☐ Participating in your local professional organization
- ☐ Organizational studies
- ☐ Implementation of social programs
- ☐ County or state organizations
- ☐ Foster care

## Chapter 2 — Private Practice

☐ Probation or dependency work
☐ Juvenile Justice
☐ Anger management
☐ Forensic psychology
☐ _____
☐ _____
☐ _____

And the list goes on. Again, the purpose of this exercise is to get you to start thinking about your ideal private practice, based on your values, beliefs, and preferences as a mental health professional.

## Fee setting

Fee setting depends on so many issues that it can get a little overwhelming to consider. There are a number of historical and theoretical issues to contemplate about money that you have already had some experience with in your education and training. However, you are now being faced with generating YOUR OWN VALUES regarding the setting of the fee.

To that end, in order to assist you in identifying and clarifying your values regarding money and fee setting, please write as many responses you can to each question. Please also write when you DISAGREE with the statements.

Describe the area(s) where you would like your practice to be. Is it in a city? Town? Is therapy accepted by the population in this area? Are there other therapists nearby? Is it near a shopping center or by doctor's offices?

# Private Practice  Chapter 2

Complete this sentence with as many responses you can come up with in 3 minutes. "Therapy should cost..."

My fee is currently

I would like my fee for individuals to be

I think _____ is too much/too little to charge for a fee.

I would like my fee for groups to be

I would feel uncomfortable charging my clients' _____/hour.

Chapter 2 — Private Practice

I am comfortable/uncomfortable working on a sliding scale.

_____
_____
_____
_____

I would base my sliding scale on

_____

When newly licensed, I feel I should charge my client(s)

_____
_____
_____
_____

I feel uncomfortable because I've been out of the therapy field for awhile, therefore I should charge my clients'

_____
_____
_____
_____

Therapy is just sitting around talking, why do therapists get paid so much?

_____

# Private Practice                    Chapter 2

_____
_____
_____

When a client comes in and tells me she/he can't afford my fee anymore, I

_____
_____
_____
_____

___ Yes ___ No   If I know my clients have insurance, I feel more comfortable with my fee because I know most of the money doesn't come out-of-pocket for my clients.

## Pager availability

Do you have a pager? Do you WANT to have a pager? How do you want to set it up when your clients are in crisis? As you do these exercises, keep in mind the potential therapeutic ramifications of your decisions. While there are no right or wrong answers per se, there will be consequences to how you set up your practice. This is why it's a good idea to get clear about the basics of how you want to set up your practice. So, here goes.

If I got paged in the middle of the night, I would feel

_____
_____
_____

## Chapter 2 — Private Practice

If one of my clients paged me in the middle of a movie or when I was out with my friends/husband/date, I would be/feel

_____

_____

_____

I agree/disagree: I mind/don't mind hearing my pager go off. It's just a natural part of being a therapist.

_____

_____

_____

When my clients are in crisis, I want them to be able to get hold of me at all times. I don't want them being redirected to another therapist or to their psychiatrist.

_____

_____

_____

_____

If a client paged me, I would feel resentful/appreciated/needed.

_____

Private Practice                                    Chapter 2

_____
_____
_____

If/when my clients page me, I charge them $__/page or __/hour.

_____
_____
_____
_____

If/when my clients page me, I don't charge them unless it takes longer than 15 minutes/20 minutes, etc.

_____
_____
_____
_____

## Phone availability

This is a BIGGIE for many therapists. What are your beliefs about phone time? Is it a freebie? Do you schedule only via phone? Do you have a time limit that you follow *before* you begin charging for phone time? (For example, 10 minutes are gratis and then a session needs to be scheduled.) Do you offer phone sessions?

I have found that many therapists remain unclear about their phone policies until their "phone boundaries" have been crossed. While there is much to be said about this style of

© Association For Advanced Training

learning, it can be EXTREMELY useful to determine your phone policy ahead of time and then provide that information to your clients during their first session. Don't wait until a potential situation or crisis emerges.

## Fee for phone sessions

I don't charge for phone sessions.

_____

_____

I charge for phone sessions that last longer than 5 minutes. I charge them at my hourly rate. I pro-rate the time.

_____

_____

_____

_____

I charge/don't charge for time spent scheduling.

_____

_____

I charge/don't charge for time spent in consultation with another professional.

_____

_____

I do/don't do phone sessions.

_____

_____

_____

List some of the potential benefits of a phone session.

_____

_____

_____

_____

List the down side to phone sessions.

_____

_____

_____

_____

## No-show policy/late cancellations/24-hour cancellation requirements

Do you have a 24-hour cancellation policy? This is pretty standard throughout the therapeutic, medical, and professional communities, but how do you manage it? How flexible (or not) is it? What is your policy for no-shows and/or cancellations at the last minute? Does it depend on

# Chapter 2 — Private Practice

the circumstances? Depend on the client? Does is somewhat depend on your relationship with the client and how long you have been working together, or is it fairly standard regardless of length of the therapeutic relationship?

Your responses to these questions should help trigger valuable answers regarding how you want to set up your cancellation/no-show policy for your practice.

I remember as an intern that I had a hard and fast rule about cancellations and no-show appointments. If you didn't give 24-hour notice, REGARDLESS OF THE REASON you would be charged. Later, as I gained more experience with myself as a therapist and as I acquired a greater understanding of the vicissitudes of life, I softened on that stance. Now, even though I would be more comfortable having a "rule," I judge each case as it comes. At the same time, I educate my clients regarding my thought processes about this issue, and I find it becomes a valuable therapeutic tool and model for **LIMIT SETTING**.

One of the most important lessons we can teach our clients is how to set limits. I have found that one of the greatest barriers to limit setting is peoples' judgment about their own limit setting and boundary making, and their mistaken belief that those limits have to "make sense" to other people, or have to at least be "reasonable."

Everyone has their own beliefs and values about what works and what doesn't work. Please remember that just because you are a neophyte in the business end of therapy doesn't mean that what you think or believe has any less value than someone who has been in private practice for 10 years. Also, you have to live within the limits and boundaries you set in your practice, so make them work for you.

Let me tell you what I tell my clients; limit setting is a PREFERENCE, nothing more. It is your desire/need/wish for things to be run a certain way that make you feel comfortable. In that sense then, there are no right answers to your policy on this issue. It is standard practice for psychiatrists to charge their clients for August vacation time, in order to "hold" their time slot. How many of us would feel comfortable with doing that? But that works in the psychiatric community. My goal is to get you to start thinking about what works FOR YOU so that you can generate a policy on this issue that is congruent with your values and belief systems.

What are your reactions to the following vignettes?

*A client calls in sick at 2:00 for a session that was originally scheduled for 6:00pm. She states she doesn't feel well and has been sick for the last five days. Do you charge her?*

*A client calls you from the side of the road and states his car broke down and it will take 45 minutes for roadside assistance to get there. This will mean that he will miss his session. Charge him? Reschedule?*

*A mother calls for the third time in six weeks to cancel the session that day for her 10-year-old daughter who has been diagnosed with an anxiety disorder. She states her daughter "just doesn't want to come, and I can't make her." How do you handle this therapeutically? What about financially? The mother also wants you to hold their session time each week at 5:00pm, which is one of your busiest and most sought after times of the day. Because the mother calls so late each week to cancel, you have been unable to re-fill that slot for the past three sessions.*

*You have been seeing a couple for the past 8 weeks. The husband is ambivalent about attending therapy and frequently the couple has called to cancel their sessions. Today at 4:00pm they have cancelled for their* scheduled session, which is tomorrow at 3:00. Do you charge them for the cancelled session? Does the fact that the notice was given with only 23 hours make a difference to you? Why or why not? Do you try to reschedule? In terms of ultimate case management issues, do you try to move them to an every other week schedule?

Your client knows your no-show and 24-hour cancellation policy. He cancels at the last minute. His insurance won't pay for no-show appointments. Do you charge him for the full session? Charge him for his portion of the regular co-pay? Attempt to reschedule? What might be some of the therapeutic ramifications for not charging him or for charging him the co-pay? (Most insurance companies have co-pay amounts between $10-30 depending on the policy. Regardless though, it is probably <u>much</u> lower than your full fee)

## Affirmations:

*I am a capable therapist.*

*I easily grasp new information and incorporate that information into my business practices.*

*I am ready for change.*

*I look forward to an exciting future in private practice.*

*Any nervousness I feel stems from the unfamiliarity of my new business, not from any incompetence on my part.*

*I am able to clarify my goals and values easily, and implement changes smoothly.*

**NOTES**

## CHAPTER 3: OFFICE SPACE AND START UP EXPENSES

You office space will say a lot about who you are as a person and as a clinician. There are numerous logistical concerns that go into this issue: whether or not to share office space, where to locate your office, how to create an office that most accurately reflects your personality and business beliefs.

Sometimes our choices about office spaces are driven by financial constraints. We may need to share an office until we are more firmly established as private practitioners. However, when the time comes for us to branch out on our own, it is important that we know what issues to consider in choosing an office. To that end, here we go with Chapter 3.

## Sharing an office

Cost – Obviously, the cost to share an office will be much less than having an office all to yourself. Depending on your area and the standards therein, office space may be charged per hour, per day or simply divided amongst the therapists. Here are some typical office-sharing scenarios.

- You may be charged $10/hour (a pretty standard fee) by the person you are subletting from and he may simply tally up your hours at the end of each month to determine what you owe him. In this scenario, the two of you may have to have your schedule posted so you can each see when the room is available and "sign up" for it.

- You and your office mate decide which days you each work and the fee is charged on a per day basis. One day might run you approximately $100-150, a second day, about the same. Again, much depends on the cost of the entire months' rent. If, for example, the rent is $600/month, then two days might run you closer to $200 for both days. (This is based on a 6-day workweek of Monday through Saturday, with each day costing $100)

- You and your office mate decide to split the office equally, either by day or by blocks of hours. Perhaps you have Mondays, Wednesdays and Fridays and he/she has Tuesdays, Thursdays and Saturdays. Or perhaps you alternate weeknights, or no one works on Mondays and you just split the Tuesday through Friday slots. Either way, the space and cost are shared equally.

Is the office you are contemplating moving into already an established office? Will you just be sharing a small amount of time in that office or is it closer to an equal split? Like any roommate situation, you have to be clear with your office mate about the logistics of the sharing of space. Let's say you are moving into an already established office. Will you be able to help decorate it? Is there anywhere to put your books or plants? Is that important to you? Does the office come "as is" with an expectation that you will not add anything to its décor or ambiance? Is participation in the décor important to you?

If the office is a new venture for the two or three of you, will you share start-up costs? Who will buy and own the furniture? What happens if one of you leaves? Frequently, when the situation in a new start-up, one of the group will opt to buy the furniture. Of course, this means that he/she will have the greater say on what style etc. and, of course, he/she will own the furniture should your office sharing situation break up.

Again though, as with many of these scenarios, all of it is negotiable. You may all chip in to buy the furniture and then have the partners pay you back a prorated amount when you leave. You may not care about the furniture and its style. It may not matter to you about wall prints and bookshelf space and potted plants. What's important is for you to know what you want and then to ask for what you need.

## Phones

Sharing a phone: This gets a bit complicated for obvious reasons. My recommendation is that, in regards to sharing a phone with an office mate - DON'T. There are so many ways to have your own phone, that this scenario shouldn't really be a necessity. With the advent of cellular phones, you wouldn't even have to get an extra phone line put in if you two (or three) wanted your own phone numbers. Simply decide who will have the "office line" and the other person(s) could have a completely independent line via their cell phone. And the cost? About the same, and this way you avoid the entire hullabaloo of whose long distance call this is, who wants call forwarding and who doesn't, etc. Also, I can't even begin to address the tax issues when you and your

# Chapter 3 — Private Practice

office mates share a line and have to divvy-up the long distance charges.

It also gets into a very tricky confidentiality issue if you opt to have call waiting. What if one therapist is on the line on a phone session and call waiting comes through for the other therapist? Get it? Will it dump automatically to voice mail?

The better way to deal with phone situations is, each therapist in the office gets their own line and/or there is one "office" line that takes care of the voicemail scenarios and other calls are done via cell phone. Also makes it nice and tidy when billing comes around. Believe me, you will have plenty to deal with that's complicated enough, without adding in the unnecessary burden of sharing a phone.

## Scheduling - on an office master or set days and times?

Scheduling is a fairly straightforward endeavor. You can simply post a "master calendar." Once you do that, there are several ways to manage the time slots:

- ☐ Each person signs up for their needed time.
- ☐ You all decide what "general times" you want and are free to fill in for those times at will. Any deviation then requires a phone call to the other person to see if their usually designated time is available for you. For example, let's say you and Janet share space and you have decided that, in general, Janet will occupy Tuesday and Thursday mornings and early afternoons until 2:30pm, and you will take the Tuesday and Thursday evenings from 3:00 'till 10:00pm. But say one of your clients is in a jam time-wise and can only come in next week at 11:00am on Tuesday morning. Well, simply call Janet and see if she is seeing clients

at 11:00. If it's available then take that time.

This kind of scheduling works really well **ONLY** if you and Janet have a cooperative working relationship. I'm sure you could imagine the possible not-so-pleasant scenarios. Janet asks you for your 6:00pm time slot every Tuesday and Thursday, which is one of you most prized time slots. You only *occasionally* ask for leeway but she seems to ask for *constant* leeway. It's a tough one, which is why many therapists prefer to do the more straightforward route of simply having pre-assigned days and time, with no deviation from the norm except in cases of emergency. You decide. Again, much depends on your relationship with your office mate.

If you don't know your office mate well, then it is best to set things up as much as you can at the beginning of the relationship. It's much easier to straighten out differences that have already been discussed previously than to be in the position to have to correct/clarify/take a stand on something further down the road.

☐ Or, you each sign up for and only pay for the hours you use the office. If there is any difference at the end of the month between what each of you have kicked in and what is owed for rent it is split between the two of you. Again, much is dependent on having a good relationship with your office mate. A good "sharing session" early on will payoff in the long-run, and help you and your partner avoid unnecessary snafus in the running of your practices.

## Renting by the hour

Renting by the hour is probably the most cost effective way of having office space if you are not planning on working full-time as a therapist. Depending on your area, the cost per hour can run you in the $8.00-12.00-ish range. Also, renting by the hour can save you on furnishing expenses, because, in general, you would be renting from an already established professional.

The down side is that, again, you have less flexibility regarding time and décor. However, if you are just starting out, or if you have decided on a "cap" for your business practice that looks more like a part-time gig, then renting by the hour may be just the ticket for you.

Many therapists have more than one office. If you are at a point in your professional career that you are able to have two different offices in two different cities, then this book probably found its way to you through a friend of a friend. However, I would like the "new-bees" to know that this is a fairly common trend in therapeutic circles, so that they know that there are <u>many</u> therapists out there who might be seeking part-time office mates.

There is one significant potential problem associated with sharing an office with one or more other mental health professionals and that is this: if, heaven forbid, there should ever be a legal entanglement, you DO NOT want to be perceived as having a "group" practice just because you share office space. You need to be clear that you are the "Sole Proprietor" of your business who happens to share the physical office space with another therapist. You do not share business practices, you are not privy to your office mates' decision-making on cases and you would therefore have no knowledge of nor would you condone any illegal or unethical thing your office mate may have allegedly been involved in. (wow, nothing like ending a difficult legalese paragraph with a preposition; I'm sure my English teacher is turning over in his grave)

Let's say your office mate gets himself into a spot of trouble ethically or legally, and someone is looking to make him pay. The opposing lawyers will first go after your office mate and his insurance company. Perhaps having done that, they now start looking for additional responsible parties. Well, if you are perceived to be in a group practice with this shenanigan-maker, they will try to come after YOU. (And, of course, your insurance carrier) However, if it is clear that you two merely SHARE PHYSICAL OFFICE SPACE, it will be a dead end moot point.

Again, in all of your documentation business-wise, you MUST be clear that you share an office ONLY. I couldn't be more serious about this issue. Look, there is enough that we have to deal with as mental health practitioners, and having an inadvertent misperception that leads to legal hassles just shouldn't be one of them.

So, how do you make this clear? Simple.

> Make sure that you sign a lease of some sort with your office mate. It can be as informal as you would like, but it should be clearly delineated that you are the leasor and the other person is the leasee.

> Clarify <u>in writing</u> how much each of you will be kicking in regarding office supplies, furniture, sundries, phones etc.

> If you choose to do professional consultation with your office mate, document it that same way you would with any other professional, i.e., make a note in your day book about a lunch appointment, consultation, or professional meeting. DON'T just "run something by

him" in the hallways until pretty soon it DOES seem like you two are running a practice together.

> Think about it from the "other point of view". Ask yourself, "is there anything about the way I interact with my office mate that could be construed as the two of us running a group practice, rather than each of us running our own businesses?" I realize it is a somewhat cumbersome question, but I think it's important to be extremely specific when it comes to legal issues.

> Make your nameplates separate. For example, list yourself, Angela Mohan, MA, MFT and then list your office mate, **Jennie Jones**, License Unknown, on a different line or with a different identification panel. DON'T put Angela Mohan and **Jennie Jones**. The latter appears to be the shared business of Ms. Mohan and Ms. Jones; the former appears to be the separate offices of Ms. Mohan and Ms. **Jones**.

> Don't get shared office stationary with a logo or shared name on it, "Anywhere, USA Counseling Services" unless you are in a partnership situation with the other people in your office. Again, this not only *implies* partnership, it actually *states* it.

> When you file for a "fictitious business name", (or a "doing business as" name), you establish for yourself legal standing as a separate entity, and that should suffice for the clarification needed to establish that you were NOT doing business with or IN business with your office mate.

> As part of your new client intake, provide each client with a statement that advises them that you are a sole proprietor and that each person with the office is a sole proprietor. Have your client(s) sign and date this

statement. You can include this in your general business practices information sheet or office policy handout.

So that's that. Now, don't let this little discussion scare you. The fact is, there will always be people out there who will try to take advantage where there is none to take. We all know this. What's more important to know however, is how to protect ourselves from unnecessary hoopla. You know the drill; "an ounce of prevention, blah blah blah"

For further discussion of this issue, I would refer you to your local, state or nationwide organization's legal department. Once you are a member, you can call them with questions and their legal staff will assist you gratis.

## Having your own office

Let's talk for a minute about having your own office. First off, it can feel rather daunting to contemplate having your own space. There are the obvious financial issues attached to having your own space, as well as the emotional and developmental issues attendant in this big move.

But let's take it one step at a time. The first issue is cost. Having your own office is generally more expensive than sharing space with another professional. You'll have to pay rent per month, plus whatever utilities expenses there are. However, if your lease allows it, you can sublet your office to another therapist in order to defray the costs of having your own office.

On the other hand, having your own office means that you, and you alone, are in charge of how that office is presented. Many people just starting out in business as a private practice mental health professional prefer to sublet from another therapist until they have gotten on their feet financially.

So, you can either have your own office, all to yourself, or sublet your office to help with your financial nut.

If you choose to have your own office, there are a number of considerations that I've listed below that might help you in thinking about office space.

## Safety issues

There are a couple of safety issues to keep in mind, whether you are subletting or getting your own office.

Make sure there is adequate lighting in the building. Before you sign your life away on some lease, go to the office building at night. Walk around. Do you feel safe there? Would your clients feel safe coming to an evening appointment? Is the building well lit in general? What about the hallways? And the parking lot? Is there good lighting, safe walkways, room between the cars and bushes? Do you need to prop open the outside door after hours for your later clients? Is there a buzzer system in case the door prop gets pushed to the side? Is your office close enough to the main front door that you would be able to hear if your client was stuck outside?

They may seem like picayune things, but they are important to your clients, and therefore, to your practice. Clients come to therapy for many things, but being frightened by the office set-up just isn't one of them. Walk your office corridors with an eye to the smallest detail of safety and a feeling of security.

Chapter 3                                          Private Practice

I think a waiting room is very important/not important because

I think the following things are important to have in a waiting room:

- ☐ Comfortable couches
- ☐ Single chairs
- ☐ Magazines
- ☐ Fresh flowers
- ☐ A clearly marked bathroom key
- ☐ Therapeutic pictures/posters/quotes posted throughout the room
- ☐ Therapy books/a lending library
- ☐ Bottled water
- ☐ "Coffee table books"
- ☐ Music
- ☐ Writing paper and pens
- ☐ Plants
- ☐ A running water fountain
- ☐ Business cards

Which of these items would you agree are necessary for the running of your business? Which would you delete? Well then, go ahead. Do what few therapists are willing/able to do after 18 years of education, <u>mark up the book</u>. That's right, put a big fat line through the items that you KNOW you could live without. And how about circling the ones you like? Go for it. This is **YOUR** handbook, your special guide to what works and what doesn't work for you in your new business venture. Be bold. Deface that textbook. (I can promise that you will **not** be visited by the Ghosts of Education Past in the middle of the night wagging bony fingers at you and threatening you with expulsion and, heaven forbid, an "F" on your project. You can do it)

## Your physical office space

Again, how you choose to set up your physical office space will have much to do with whom you choose to be as a therapist and your resources to create that for yourself. Some people place a great emphasis on how their room looks, and believe that this, in great part, determines what kinds of clients they will be serving and how they come across as clinicians. Others believe that an office should be as "tabula rasa" as possible, in order to allow the therapy to be about something *other* than the décor.

Again, you guessed it; there are no right or wrong answers. I believe you should have an office that reflects who you are, both as a person and as a clinician. Like colors? Add 'em in. Go for the more esoteric decorations and wall hangings? What harm could it do? Our clients are looking for us to be real-live human beings, not simply beige automatons, and our offices are one of the places that this is reflected.

Now, some of your decision-making about your office will obviously depend on the kind of therapy you do. Again, think children's play room, grief work, art therapy, etc. And, some of what you choose will be dependent on your theoretical orientation and your beliefs about what makes a healing environment. But the deal is, you decide.

Pay attention to how you feel in your gut when you read these next vignettes.

# Chapter 3 — Private Practice

*You walk into a room. It is beige, with lots of doctor-style waiting room chairs. There are magazines on the tables and Musak overhead. There is nothing that would differentiate this room from a hundred other waiting rooms you've been in.*

*You walk into a room (alright already, enough with the walking). It is filled with lively oldies music. The walls are painted several muted colors, the chairs are fat, fluffy and comfortable, and there are a number of wall prints and sayings throughout the place. You can't look anywhere without seeing some piece of information or framed saying.*

*You walk into a room. (Groundhog Day, anyone?) There is New Age music on the stereo, a faint scent of incense burning, books on the shelves and hot tea waiting to be poured. You feel like whispering it's so quiet.*

*You walk into a room. The walls are deep maroon, taupe and beige. The chairs and couches are comfortable and there are intricate patterned designs on all of the throw pillows and on the therapist's chair. You feel like you've just stepped into a different world where there is a canopy hanging in the office, masks on several of the walls, and knick-knacks from different countries on the bookshelves.*

So, what did you think? What was your reaction to each of the offices? Did some make you think, "yes, that's what an office should be" and other's make you wonder what the practitioner was thinking? Listen to yourself. This is VALUABLE information. This will give you an idea of what works best for you in an office space.

## Isolation

Watch for this wicked therapy bug-a-boo. Do whatever you can to keep yourself from professional and personal isolation. We'll talk more about this in the chapter entitled, "Self Care", but for now suffice it to say that you MUST NOT allow yourself to become isolated as a therapist. It's way too easy considering the basic make-up of our professions. So be diligent about keeping this one at bay. Join professional organizations, have regularly scheduled peer supervision, and have lunch weekly with building mates. Whatever it is, do it. This is the single most important contributing factor that leads to therapist burnout, so catch it early. (More on this topic later in Chapter 8, "Self Care")

## Tenant improvements (e.g., carpet, paint)

Frequently, first time renters or leasers don't know that, many times, buildings have allotted each tenant a certain amount of money for "tenant improvements." Now, each building is different, (and some don't even have a cache for tenant improvements) but many will allow you a certain amount of money to change or improve your working space. You might be able to request a fresh coat of paint, choose a new color of paint, put up a new wall, sound proof the doorways, partition off an area to make it into a private office for your desk, choose new carpeting, or get new blinds. The point is if you don't know about tenant improvements, you won't know to ask about them. So check it out.

## Leasing vs. renting

I'm sure you all know the difference between renting and leasing. The same that would apply for an apartment building goes for an office building. Rentals are month-to-month, rent can be raised (with due notice) at will, and either party can give a one-month notice to vacate at any time. Leasing generally involves a yearlong or two-year commitment, rent cannot be raised within that period of time, (except as previously agreed upon by both parties at the time of leasing signature) and "notice" is not really notice. You have a contract, when that contract is up, you can re-up for the space or find another office.

There are pros and cons to both. Some newbies in the business think it's safer to get a month-to-month deal so that they can get out of it faster if need be. (Personally, I think this just hexes your business before you even get started) Others like the freedom renting allows. Still others wouldn't dream of doing anything other than a lease. They like the long-term aspect of it; it feels more permanent. And, many therapists don't want to move their offices because of the high rate of client attrition involved in moving one's space. You decide what's best for you.

## Cleaning crew/arrangements

Be sure, whichever plan you choose (renting or leasing) that you find out what their policy/deal is regarding cleaning. Who keeps up the grounds? Office? Common areas? Most places, regardless of the types of agreement you have, will provide all of the grounds keeping and general up-keep for the outside of the office and the office building. You then are responsible for your individual office. But, there are just as many who do the whole deal. Check so you know.

# Private Practice · Chapter 3

## Water/electricity/air conditioning/heat

Be sure not to overlook this important aspect of an office. If you are in a suite of offices, controlled by a single heat/air conditioning console, then you'd best be sure to check on what the temperature is usually set at.

What would it be like for you to do therapy and feel so hot you feel like your suffocating? Or to feel so cold you feel like you have to provide your clients with throw blankets when they come to see you?

Find out what temperature works for you and then what temperature the console is set. This could be a deal-breaker, so heads up.

Note: some office buildings are set up NOT to provide heat or air conditioning on the weekends and/or after "traditional" business hours of 8:00am-5:00pm. Be sure you know the situation before you sign the lease. If you don't do much work "after" hours, then it shouldn't be a problem. If you do work after hours, then decide if you can live with this condition. If you can, factor in buying a space heater and/or fan for the off hours.

## Start-up expenses

### Office space - per/hour or first and last

I think we've pretty much covered this in the section on how to set up your office and whether or not to share office space. In terms of start-up expenses, the key here is to know that you can rent space by the hour from an already established practitioner, or you can go for having your own office and paying the full pop each month. The key is to remember that, in terms of start-up expenses, if you go for having your own office space, you will also have to budget for the whole first/last/security deal that is attendant on new rental leases.

## **Furniture**

Furniture. We will be dealing with all of the in's and out's of furniture decision-making and acquisition in the following chapter on Office Equipment and furniture. For the purposes of THIS chapter (on start-up expenses only), I would like you to consider the following:

If you choose to share an office and it is already furnished, then you can skip this section en masse.

If you choose to go in with a partner it doesn't matter if that partner is simply sharing office space with you or the two of you are going to be a "Partnership" in terms of start-up furniture expenses. Somehow the two of you will decide on how to split up the costs of the furniture in the office. Maybe one of you has greater financial resources and is willing to furnish the place, then the only thing the two of you need to decide is what kind of furniture to have. Or maybe you believe that he/she who pays, decides. Also fine, just keep in mind to <u>choose</u> that decision rather than making an assumption about how things are going to work.

If you choose to share an office and it is NOT furnished, and the two of you are going to be deciding all of the furniture issues together, then check out the next chapter.

If you are going to have an office to yourself, then there are numerous furniture issues to consider, so again, refer to the next chapter.

## Business cards

Here's the deal with business cards. They are your representatives out there in the world for you. They are your first line of defense against complete professional oblivion. They speak of who you are as a clinician. While all of this is true and important and sound business-wise, it is also true that YOU CAN CHANGE THEM WHENEVER YOU WANT. Look guys, our professional identity changes and grows and develops as we spend time in our chosen field. What seems "perfect" as a fledgling therapist may make our professional toes curl five years later. We may ask ourselves, "What was I thinking?" when we look back at our cherished first business card with the sweet bunnies on it. Or we may be clear about how we represent ourselves and have very little need to change our cards as time goes by. Either way, please remember that, again, YOU CAN CHANGE THEM WHENEVER YOU WANT.

I can't tell you how many people I know that should be changing their cards based on how they look when they are handing them out. They don't look you in the eye, they seem embarrassed by them, they mumble when they hand them to you. C'mon guys! If this is you, then get off your duff, find the money and change those cards!!! Yes it may be more than you want to spend, especially considering that you're thinking, "I already have cards, I'll order different ones when I get rid of these thousand", but remember that these cards stand in your stead when you are not around to represent yourself in the flesh. Don't allow them to misrepresent you. Okay? Okay.

P.S. A word on business cards. MAKE SURE YOU PROOF THEM before you pay for them. Most places take your order and have you pay for them when you come back for the finished product. This is great because you then should have the opportunity to proof the cards before they are actually

# Chapter 3 — Private Practice

printed. Be careful nevertheless. Some places take down the information you give them and immediately go into printing them. You may be thinking there will be a separate proof to be viewed at a later date and they are just printing them as is. Then changing the possibly wrong cards is like moving heaven and earth. So please remember that you need to see the "finished proof" before you give your final ok on the order.

## Calendar/palm pilot

You must have a calendar of sorts, no matter how small or how large and detailed it is. You must have a place to record your appointments and your other professional meetings and luncheons etc. You can do this in a traditional paper calendar or on a palm pilot. Go with whatever works for you. If you love the technical aspects of the palm pilot, then go for it. If you tend to be more old-fashioned and like to see your week laid out for you visually, then go for the more traditional paper and pen mode.

My only caution in terms of getting a palm pilot is this: if you have never used one and you don't tend to be technically literate, then perhaps you might want to incorporate the palm pilot into you professional life at a later date. There is such a high learning curve in starting your own business and putting out the resources financially, emotionally and logistically that, if you can save yourself some brain cells and energy in this area, then I recommend that you do so. Get the palm pilot _after_ you've set up and mastered your office space, equipment, forms and office policies. Then it'll be the fun everyone says it is, instead of an unnecessary hassle just to locate your day's schedule.

## Business stationary/letterhead

Some would say this is a "must have" and others might take a pass on this initially in the interest of saving money and avoiding hassles. I think the key is again determining how much you are going to be dealing with "the public" in terms of letters, memo's, super bills, etc.

This is definitely an expense that can wait. If you have a computer, or even access to one, you can create your own letterhead on Word or any other related program. If you are uninterested in letterhead per se, then simply put all relevant information in a business style format and be done with it. Letterhead becomes more of an issue when you have a logo of some type or when you are doing a lot of correspondence right out of the gate. And the fact is, most us aren't in that position. In general, correspondence and the need for "official letterhead" come a bit later, after we've established ourselves somewhat. So, toss this, or at least put it on the back burner for the time being if you are able.

## Office "incidentals"

Keep in mind that you may be able to raid your home supplies for some of these items, so please don't think that this is a "must have" list before you get started in your private practice. All are useful but not absolutely vital to the running of your business, at least initially.

- Stapler
- Files with ecco fasteners
- Pens
- Pencils
- Tape
- 2 or 3 hole punch

- Paper clips
- Rubber bands
- White-out
- Post-its
- Paper

## *Affirmations:*

*I have enough money to get started in my new business.*

*I trust that I have made adequate preparations financially for the move to my new office.*

*I am well organized and accomplish my many business tasks with ease and grace.*

*My office is comfortable and reflects who I am as a therapist to my clients.*

*I feel safe in my office. My needs are met professionally in my office space.*

*I ask for what I want from my landlord with ease and assurance that my wishes will be responded to.*

**NOTES**

# CHAPTER 4: EQUIPMENT/FURNITURE

There are a couple different schools of thought on the whole issue of office equipment. One generally says you DON'T need all this stuff to get started, and the other says, (surprise of all surprises), that you DO need all this stuff to get started. So, let's see if we can figure it out together.

## Equipment

### Telephones and answering machines/voicemail

If you are going to be a private practice therapist, then a phone is an absolute necessity. While it doesn't matter what kind of phone you get (land line or cell) what DOES matter is that it is a separate line from your home or pre-existing work line.

Many therapists who are just starting out as private practice clinicians are tempted to use their already existing "work phone" as their private practice office phone numbers.

However, there are a number of possible conflict of interest issues there. As tempting as it may be to save money by using an already existing line, get a separate line if you are going to start work as a private practice clinician.

That being said, there are lots of ways to do this. You can have an actual land-locked phone line installed by your local phone company that has a phone jack and a phone attached in a physical office. You can then decide on voicemail or an answering machine to deal with phone messages.

Or, you can have a cell phone that has voicemail attached to it and never ever have a land-locked phone line going to a physical office space. More and more people are choosing this option these days because they like the convenience of it, because they may have more than one office space, because they have a cell phone anyway and why then have a landline to boot?

In addition, with the competitive market being what it is, you can get really terrific deals on minutes, voicemail, long-distance etc. You also get an itemized bill every month, which is great for tax purposes.

If you decide to go with the traditional "land line," remember that you will have to get either voicemail attached to your phone number, or purchase an answering machine. (If you opt for the latter, be sure to get an answering machine with "remote access" as a feature. This allows you to check your messages from outside of your office, you know, call in from home etc. Without remote access, you MUST be in your physical office in order to check your messages)

You may choose to get a cell phone as your primary business line. If you do, it means that your office phone number will remain the same, even if you change office spaces. (And clients tend to keep our business cards with phone numbers with them, and they will therefore be able to reconnect with you in the future even if you've moved cross town) The down side to the cell phone set up is that you are not listed in the phone book or yellow pages.

Either way, like I said before, YOU HAVE GOT TO HAVE A PHONE before you do almost anything else in this business. So, decide on whatever option works best for you and go with it.

## Fax machines

Here the issue is not so cut and dry. Whether or not you have a fax machine depends in great part on whether or not you need one. (I know, well, DUH, but you would be surprised at how many people <u>think</u> they need a fax machine when in reality they only use it once a month.) So, first thing to do is to think about how much you currently use or how much you think you'll be using a fax machine. Next question, can you use the fax at the local copier for your faxing needs? Do you need to have access to someone being able to fax you possibly confidential information? How much are you planning on dealing with insurance companies?

So just think about it. And again, you may find that you don't need a fax machine immediately, but that after the first year you <u>do</u> need one. Well then, get one next year, but at least it will save you that first year when start-up expenses can be so steep.

## Pagers

Here's yet another difference among professionals. Some private practice practitioners swear by their pagers and, like the American Express card, would never leave home without it. Other's don't really use pagers and prefer to route everything through their cell phones and voice-mail options.

The important thing to remember is this: whatever you decide, you must simply have a way in which you deal with client emergencies, and that way must be clear to all of your clients. Again, much of your decision-making on this issue will depend on how you choose to do business and who you are in the world as a therapist.

Don't want to carry a pager? Then make sure your voice-mail message states what your client's can do in case of an emergency. Call such and such number, call 911, or call a designated on-call therapist. Some therapists don't carry pagers because they have trained their clients to not expect a pager. They make emergency plans and have those plans clearly spelled out on their messages, but those plans don't involve being able to get hold of that therapist 24/7. There is nothing wrong with this school of thought, although this scenario is often met with looks of horror by our more traditional therapists who believe that being available 24/7 is part of what they signed up for, and is an integral part of the healing process for their clients.

Are you one of the one's who wants to carry a pager? Well then the only thing you have to consider is whether or not the pager works statewide, nationally, or just locally. That's just a simple phone call away to your pager provider for that answer, and its okay if it doesn't work in the larger geographical picture. Again, the only issue is to be aware of your pager limits so that you can make plans if you'll be out of town, out of the area or out of state. Conversely, you'll need to find out if your pager will register if <u>your client</u> is out of the area or out of state. Some pagers will register an out of the area call and some won't, so just find out which yours is and plan accordingly.

Again, most of this kind of decision-making depends on your theoretical orientation and your beliefs about what makes therapy work. My point here is to get you to make a

CURRENT decision about what works for you, based on your beliefs after having done thousands and thousands of hours of work in this field. Don't just go with what "everyone" does, or what you were trained to do at the counseling center where you earned your hours. Who you choose to be as a private practice therapist may very well be different than who you were as an intern.

And finally, what do I always say? YOU CAN CHANGE YOUR MIND about what works for you. Tried the pager route and it doesn't work for you? Then simply go back, re-educate your existing clients, set policy for your new clients as they come in and implement the new regime. You can do this over the course of several months if need be, until your old clients get the hang of the new system, but it certainly can be done.

## Computer

Okay, computers. You want one? Get one. Do you <u>need</u> one? Not especially. Now remember, I'm gearing this entire book to address the needs and issues of the *first time or expanding* practitioner. That being the case, my assumption is that you may not be currently rolling in the dough, and that being "thrifty" has become a character trait that you want to embrace. A computer would be nice, but it is not necessary.

Many people have a computer at home, and you can do much of your computer work there until such time as you can afford one for your office. The key thing to remember about doing private practice work on a home computer is that you need to be particularly careful about confidentiality issues. File your session notes in a "locking" document, save the billing to a floppy and then keep it under lock and key, etc.

If you DO have the $$ for a computer, you might consider a Laptop which can move between your office and your home. (A nice 2 for 1 deal!) Either way, spending wise you're looking at around $600-$1,000 for a desktop computer and probably around $900-$1,500 for a Laptop. Much depends on which model, what amenities, programs, gadgets are included etc. I won't even TRY to go into the whys and wherefores of computer buying, better to save that subject for a non-technophobe. Ask around, check out some local office supply and computer stores and take it from there.

## Locking filing cabinet

A must for every new practitioner, no matter how fledgling your practice. What do you need? At the very least you need to have a locking file cabinet in your main office, (not waiting room). It is generally recommended though, that you have a locking file cabinet behind an <u>additionally</u> locking door. That is, your file cabinet would go in your office, which would be locked separately from your waiting room. That makes three locks before some hooligan could access your files; the main office door lock which leads into your waiting room, the next-door lock that would lead you to the session room, and the locking file cabinet. Just so you know, the second set of door locks is merely a legal recommendation, not a legal necessity.

## Door plaque/name in building directory

Depends on your office building. Some require your name rank and serial number to be posted at their directory as well as on your door, but most give you the option. I'd love to give you a ballpark figure as to how much this might run you, but the prices vary so much that it defies delineation. I've seen directory and name plaques cost as little as $50.00

and as much as $300.00. These are, in general, one time fees, and most places will allow you to take your plaque with you when you leave. Of course, there is no guarantee, (and very little likelihood) that the plaque will fit your *next* office, but it's the thought that counts, right?

Anyway, these vary from building to building, and much depends on the kind of building and the area where you've chosen to practice. A plaque in a Beverly Hills building will likely be more expensive than one in Tiny-Town U.S.A.

A reiterated caution: remember the deal with <u>appearing</u> to share a practice with another therapist? Be wise about this name plaque issue. If you are sharing an office with another therapist, but you are NOT sharing a practice, then have the plaques printed up separately, or be sure that each of your names is listed on a separate line. If that is impossible, than be sure to have your names separated by a comma, not an "and."

   Jane Centered, PhD, John Differentiated, LCSW

   rather than Jane Centered, PhD <u>and</u> John Differentiated, LCSW

The second gives the appearance that Jane and John are in business together and that they share a practice, rather than that they simply share office space. This may seem extraordinarily picayune, but it's important in case, heaven forbid, Jane or John get their little selves into legal trouble and the lawyers come knocking at your door looking to cash in on your lucrative practice.

## Palm Pilot vs. pen and paper

Your choice. Technically oriented? Then have at the Palm Pilot. Old-fashioned and still trying to figure out the remote control for your VCR? Then stick with pen and paper. And don't let any of those "techies" convince you that you HAVE to use a Palm Pilot. Sure they've got great bells and whistles, but you're going to be dealing with such a steep learning curve getting your business off the ground that you don't really need the psychosis of unnecessary paraphernalia. Give yourself a break. This whole "being in business for yourself" can really take it out of you, and there's simply no use making yourself feel like a technical Neanderthal for no good reason.

## Furniture

### Couches vs. chairs

Lots and lots of people have opinions about what your office should look like, what creates an ideal "therapeutic environment" blah blah blah, but I'm going to give you the real deal. Ready?

The deal with your office furniture is, IT'S TOTALLY UP TO YOU. Want to have couches? Go for it. Chairs suit you better? Fly, be free. Going for the combo look? Have a great time.

C'mon everyone, I know you've already gotten the message six different ways to Sunday. THERE IS NO ONE WAY (and certainly no "right" way) to do things when it comes to your private practice. I know the "old school" thinking was "go with beige", but times have changed, and now the most important aspect of your office is how comfortable and happy you are in it.

So let yourself go. If you like minimalist, do minimalist. Prefer plush, then fluff away. But just buy whatever fits for you.

And of course, you'll have to keep the space constraints in mind. Be sure to MEASURE before you buy. (I mean it. Bring a measuring tape with you to the store when you're buying office furniture. This will save you the hassle of returning that item when it doesn't fit into the space you thought it would.)

If you should choose to go for sofas, then keep several things in mind. Take a look at who your clients tend to be demographically. If you see populations like teenagers, couple's or families with small children then you should consider the "wearability" of the couch. (This includes the durability and clean-ability of the fabric on your couch) It may make better sense to you to spend less on your couches with the thought that you will replace your couches every few years because you have clients that might be "hard" on your furniture. On the other hand, if you primarily see adults, and have a no eating/no drinking policy for your sessions, you might opt for the higher end couch that will last longer and is not required to be as "durable."

## Ergonomic/special chairs

Many therapists prefer to have their own designated chair and some go for the ergonomically correct chairs to save wear and tear on their bodies in the long run. It's tough sitting for most of the day, so do whatever you have to do to make that a tolerable and/or pleasant experience.

Ergonomically designed chairs cost a bit more (a slight understatement but I don't want to scare you away from even considering it) but are worth it in the long run, and clinicians who have them swear by them.

Even if you don't choose an ergonomically correct chair, be sure that the chair you DO choose fits you well. Sit it in, cross your legs, if you take notes in session, bring a clipboard with you to see if the chair would allow you to take notes easily. Check out the armrests. I know you will probably not feel comfortable sitting in it in the store for too long, but do what you can to make sure it's a chair you'll want to be spending some time in.

## Lamps-floor and table

Much depends on your office set up, but you'll probably need at least one side table lamp and a few floor lights. You can get those nice stand up lamps starting at $20 so don't worry too much about the price here.

Also, check out your office. Does it have fluorescents and do you want to use them? Maybe you can have the building manager tone down the fluorescents by half. If not, you may want to go exclusively with separate lights.

## Coffee and end tables and waiting room furniture

Decide what "look" you want and plan accordingly. Don't think you have to limit yourself to office furniture places; check out the major department stores and specialty stores as well.

Be sure to add in delivery charges to your purchase, or see if you can borrow someone's SUV or truck to save on costs, if that's an issue.

And don't forget to MEASURE!!!

## Music system

A fairly simple "boom box" will suffice. You can either set the radio for a station that you like, or bring in CD's. Again, depends on what you want to communicate to your clients when they come to your office.

Be sure that the music and volume level fits your office. Remember, the music is for background noise, to provide a pleasant diversion to waiting, and to mask somewhat whatever is going on in your office. However, it should not be so loud that your client is tempted to sing along to the oldies while you are in session.

## Magazines

Seems like a must, doesn't it? Well, sign up for a few, and have them sent directly to your office. (Do NOT have them sent to your home and then bring them to your office yourself. Number one, you might forget to take the address tag off and now everyone knows your home address. And number two; if you want the magazines as a tax write-off, you will want to have them delivered directly to your office)

Pick magazines that you believe might interest your clientele.

Take home or donate the old issues as they are replaced by current copies of the magazines. (Mental health professionals frequently donate their old magazines to a local hospital, children's shelter, group home, convalescent home or social services office)

Some perennial favorites for waiting rooms are "People," "Time," "Newsweek," "Teen whatever" (there are so many I couldn't even begin to choose the best one), "Sports Illustrated," "Ladies Home Journal," "Readers Digest," and "Bon Appetite." Most of these have short enough articles that they can be read in 15-20 minutes and have engaging pictures in them to boot. Again, tailor your magazine choices to match your clientele.

## Desk

If you have the space for one, and you will be doing some/much of your work at the office, then a desk is a must. Find one that meets your needs, i.e., if you have a computer etc.

If you have a "loose" system of organization, or are used to keeping lots of stuff on your desk, just be cognizant of the confidentiality issues. File it, cover it, and make sure no one sees it as they are walking through your office.

## Bookshelves

Again depends on space and need. Most therapists have at least one bookshelf, the contents of which can be fairly standardized: Yalom's *Group Psychotherapy*, Napier's *The Family Crucible*.

Other therapists like to have a"lending library" for their clients and keep copies of the latest and greatest of the Self-Help books. Whichever way works for you is fine. I would recommend however that you decide on a policy about lending books to your clients BEFORE they ask you to borrow them. Maybe you would want to develop a sign in/sign out system to keep track of where your tomes are. Or perhaps you are only willing to write down the name and logistics of the book and then direct your client to the nearest bookseller. Again, whatever way works for you is perfect.

## Prints/decorations

I don't know if I've said this before, but IT'S TOTALLY UP TO YOU. Let everyone have their own opinion, you're the only one who's got to live in this place day in and day out; you might as well make it someplace that makes you happy.

## Affirmations:

*I acquire the furniture and equipment I need for my office happily.*

*I have enough money.*

*My office is a reflection of who I am as a person and as a therapist. I rejoice in the opportunity to express myself.*

**NOTES**

# CHAPTER 5: FORMS

**Intake form/client information sheet**

In general, your intake form should include name, address, phone number, (home, work and cell) emergency contacts, date of birth, social security number (frequently needed for insurance billing), any and all other insurance information, name of referral, name of doctor or psychiatrist. Finally, it should include a place for the client's signature.

Many people have their intake sheets formulated on an office document, other are less formal. Many counseling centers and clinics that employ interns will allow you to copy their intake forms when you leave, (minus of course their logo), but be sure to ask before pilfering.

If you like to send out stuff via e-mail, (newsletters, upcoming event announcements) you can also ask your clients to include their e-mail address on the intake form. Be careful though, you open up a veritable Pandora's Box of clinical issues once you start corresponding with your clients via e-mail. Be sure you have a "policy" in place BEFORE you hand out or take e-mail addresses.

## Confidentiality

In general, this is an information sheet. It should include a discussion of the parameters of therapy as it pertains to confidentiality. In other words, it's got to have the limits of confidentiality as well as the mandated reporting circumstances. Many therapists have a space at the bottom of the handout for their clients' signature. This gives clear documentation that you have provided the information to your client, and should then be copied. You keep the original and give the copy to your client.

## Consent for treatment/treatment of a minor

There is the consent for treatment and consent for the treatment of a minor: different forms.

Consent for Treatment is merely the client's consent to participate in psychotherapy. Sometimes clinicians enumerate the costs and benefits of being in therapy, (informed consent) and sometimes this form is as simple as they come: agree to be in therapy with this clinician? Well then sign on the dotted line and it's a done deal.

Treatment of a Minor is a different situation altogether. Now, different States and jurisdictions may have slightly different rules, so be sure to brush up on the ones applicable to your license, but the general rule is, whoever has the legal authority to sign for a minor to be in treatment can do so.

That may be a parent, the court systems in cases of dependency or probation cases, or a legal guardian.

Whatever it is, be sure you know who can sign BEFORE you begin treatment.

## Office policy form

This little number clarifies for your clients your business practices such as cancellation policy, phone sessions, billing, pager information, what to do in case of an emergency etc. Many therapists find it useful to give their clients a printed list of their office policies at the first session.

From a legal standpoint, this is a vital piece of information for your clients. No licensing or state Board will tell you how to set up your practice in terms of your business. There are some professional standards but the most important issue is whether or not your clients know your policies and what to do in case of an emergency.

Perhaps you are one of the people who don't carry a pager. Then your Office Policy Form needs to clearly spell out what a client needs to do in the "off" hours if they have a emergency and they can't reach you. That might include giving them hotline numbers, 911, another therapists' number who covers for you on weekends etc. Whatever it is, it needs to be clear.

Some therapists have their clients sign an acknowledgement of receipt of the form and keep a separate copy in their client file. (One copy of course going to your client)

## Release of confidential information

A MUST HAVE if you ever want to talk with anyone about your client. It should include very specific things: client's name, date of birth, the person whom you are requesting information from (or the person whom you are going to be

Chapter 5 — Private Practice

providing information to), the specific information requested, the time frame of the release, and then the signature and date of signature of your client.

Without these very specific pieces of information, the Release is not so valid, and remember, this is a HUGE legal issue, so don't mess around here. Better to be more specific as to what information is being shared than to leave any question about the release because of it being too general.

> *You are seeing a 45-year-old woman in your office who states that recently she has been extremely irritable, found herself yelling at her family and co-workers, and cries at the drop of a hat. She states that this is unusual behavior for her as she is usually considered to be pretty patient and calm. She states she has recently been laid off from her job of 15 years and thinks her marriage of 22 years has lost its vitality.*

Okay, there are some clear therapeutic issues here. Relationship stuff no doubt, job/career stuff, adjustment issues; sounds like she got hit with a bunch of things at once and is trying to regain her balance. But, she's 45, a woman, and describes her recent mood behaviors as unusual. I would want a medical evaluation pretty quickly to rule out/address the possibility that at least SOME of her stuff is hormonally based. If this woman is pre-menopausal and doesn't know it, then she's going to have a hard time in therapy if that stuff isn't assessed and addressed.

Now, regardless of your orientation and/or likes and dislikes of psychotropic medications or hormone therapies, you must recommend that this woman see a medical doctor. (Maybe NONE of it is hormonally based, but at least you'll know that after the medical exam and can proceed with therapy without a big fat question mark hanging over your clinical head)

And now we return to the Release of Confidential Information that started this whole sordid mess.

The Release in this case should include: your client's name, her date of birth, the name of the doctor or medical group you are requesting information from, her signature, date, your name, logistics, blah, blah blah. But the KEY pieces of information you would want addressed by her doctor are:

- Her current medical diagnosis (if any)
- A list of any current medications the client is taking
- Results of her physical exam, and
- Whether or not the doctor has cleared her for physical exercise (in case you want to recommend any kind of movement therapy to help her decrease her mood symptomology)

Sounds pretty clear, right? Therapy is based on a very solid foundation of CONFIDENTIALITY, without it, our therapeutic hands are tied. Any time confidentiality is at stake, be very VERY compulsive, specific, and picayune about how it gets managed.

Note: Remember to place a copy of the signed Release of confidential Information in your clients file.

## Assignment of insurance benefits

A fairly simple form. It states that the client assigns insurance benefits to you so that you can bill their insurance company. It basically keeps their signature "on file" so that you don't have to have them sign each and every billing form you send out.

It also delineates whether the insurance money reimburses the client or comes directly to you. In general, the form usually specifies that the insurance money come to you, the client only having paid their portion of the co-pay, rather than the other way around. (If you are providing your client with a super-bill and they have already paid up-front for your services, then this form is a non-issue)

## Termination/discharge letter

Let's set aside the Urban Legends about therapists who DIDN'T do this letter and then ended up in legal hell. The fact is this is an important piece of documentation regardless of the fear factor involved if you don't do it.

It is always a good idea to "cap" your time with a client officially. Certainly a termination session is the best-case scenario at the end of treatment, but we all know that sometimes that just isn't possible. Whether or not you had a termination session is beside the point. You should always write a termination statement in your notes.

The Discharge letter would be more applicable in the cases where you were unable to do a termination session with your client, or your client has simply stopped showing up for therapy. In that case, you MUST follow up with a termination/discharge letter stating that you will no longer be providing services to this person and giving them 3 referrals for counseling elsewhere.

## "What is therapy?"/informed consent

This is an optional form. Some clinicians like to "orient" their clients to the therapeutic process and give them general information about their beliefs and process of therapy. Others prefer to leave it an ongoing process with no written explanations provided ahead of time. Either way is fine. While the law says you have to clarify WHAT THERAPY IS to clients (e.g. talking about relationships, improving quality of life issues) you are not required to spell out exactly <u>how</u> you do that.

Some clinicians like to educate their clients as much as possible on the therapeutic process, with the underlying belief that the more education and information a client has, the better able they will be to make use of the therapeutic process. Others prefer to let the therapy "unfold", and find little to no value in giving their clients didactic information about therapy.

Either way is fine. The primary legal and ethical issues attached to this are that clients have to know your particular scope of practice and you have to work with the scope of your license. Simply put, you need to let your clients know what you as a clinician do from a legal standpoint in terms of Scope of Practice. MFT's and counselors specifically must work within the bounds of helping clients improve their relationships. Social workers can have a somewhat broader definition and they tend to focus their clinical attention on improving the quality of life of their clients. Psychologists are involved with broadening the general and societal knowledge of behavior and improving the conditions of the individuals and society.

Whatever it is that you do as a mental health professional, be sure that your client knows about your scope of practice when they come to you for treatment.

## Initial assessment forms

Another must. (Are you getting the feeling that paperwork can take up a large part of your practice? Well, you are certainly on the right track)

The Initial Assessment Form is similar to a Client Information Form or Intake Form but it frequently also includes your initial assessment of the presenting problems, issues facing this client, and beginning treatment plan.

There is no specific or right way to do this form. Combine the two or not, it really doesn't matter. Just make sure you have a complete initial "picture" of your client.

## Mental Status Examination

Nothing necessarily formal is needed here. Do the Mental Health Examination in whatever stylized way works for you, and then document it, either as a separate form or in your session notes. Some clinicians prefer a MSE that is a bunch of check boxes, some prefer the longhand version.

## Personal history forms

These would be expanded versions of your Initial Intake Forms. They would include a more complete history and questions such as:

- Have you ever been in therapy before?
- Why are you seeking treatment now?
- Childhood and developmental history
- Relationship history
- Mood questionnaire
- Job/Career history
- Substance use history

The counseling center where you did your hours might give you permission to use their form, or another therapist you know might have a special form that they find useful. Just be sure to check on copyright issues before you copy someone else's form. No use taking so much time on the legal and ethical side of a therapy practice and then blowing it on something like copyright infringement.

Note: A lot of therapists make up their own forms, including only what information they find relevant to their practices. They frequently create the forms on a computer program and there is usually no copyright issue. So, check around with some of your "therapy buddies" and ask them to use some of their forms when you're just getting started. Chances are, later in your practice you will want to tailor those same forms to fit your own practice, but in the meantime, you'll have something to work with.

## Treatment form

This form should include initial assessment, diagnosis, and treatment plan. It should then be updated to include progress in treatment and any change in diagnosis. Many clinicians include treatment issues in the body of their session notes, which is fine. Just be sure you can easily access the client's overall treatment goals so that you can assist yourself in staying on track.

## Session/progress notes

Look around if you don't already have a method you like for taking session notes. In the medical community, they follow a strict S.O.A.P. method of progress notes, S -subjective, O - Objective, A - Assessment, and P - Prognosis or Plan. Some therapists have modified this with the additional N - Narrative and I - Interventions. Broken down, it would look something like this:

**Narrative** – Includes what the client tells about themselves and the specifics of their lives. (Last week my daughter broke her leg, I think I might be getting laid off, my brother-in-law is coming to visit, etc.)

**Subjective** – What the client reports about how they have felt throughout the week or insights/commentary about how they are doing internally, what they think about what is going on for them, what they report about their lives ("I still feel stuck", "I can't seem to be able to make a decision about her", "I'm so frustrated during the week I could just scream", "I just can't seem to fall asleep at night")

**Objective** – What you see, what you observe of the client in the room with you, (they appeared teary eyed, flat affect, very animated, etc.)

**Intervention** – What you DID in the room or what homework you gave to your client for the upcoming week, (reframed their negative view of themselves, suggested they take a walk by the beach during the week in order to relax, gave stem-sentence completion homework, intervened when client began negative self-talk in session, etc.)

**Assessment** – How is the client currently doing in terms of therapeutic goals? (They appear to understand and the grief process, they have made strides in their self-care skills, they are markedly less depressed, they have continued to follow the recommendations of their psychiatrist regarding psychotropic medications, they were able to notice when their thoughts have exacerbated and/or intensified their mood)

**Plan** – What is on the agenda in future sessions? What do you want to put on your list of things to focus on during the upcoming sessions? (Move from an intellectual understanding of grief to affective expressions of grief, assist client in understanding the role her family of origin played in the development of her core beliefs, assist client in improved skills acquisition for more effective mood management, etc.)

Take a look at this sample of a client session note.

> A couple, Wally and June, come to see you. Their third child has recently gone off to college and they have a lot of time on their hands. He says she is crowding him and she says he is distancing from her, and is afraid he is having an affair. Wally used to coach his son's little league team and June used to be actively involved in PTA and school volunteer activities.

Let's just say for the purposes of session note-taking that the goals of therapy include educating the couple on the developmental life cycle they are experiencing, increasing their communication skills, and helping both to manage, structure and enhance their time as a couple vs. as a large family unit.

Session notes after a few months might look like this:

### N - Narrative

Wally states that the week has gone "better." June agrees with him, although neither could comment on why that was the case. June states they are looking forward to their sons coming home for the holidays. Wally states he and June had "date night" as discussed the previous week in session

### S - Subjective

June states she is still feeling sad and still a little bit angry that Wally isn't spending more time with her, Wally states he is trying but still feels like June is relying on him for "everything" and feels suffocated, June says she is finding it easier to get together with her girlfriends

## O - Objective

Wally and June appeared less emotionally volatile this session; they were able to discuss their issues more calmly and are better able to utilize reflective listening skills when coached to do so in session

## I - Interventions

Refocused June on what she could do outside of the home and the relationship to get her social needs met, did role play with both to assist in understanding their partners' point of view, gave information sheet on the developmental life cycle of families, asked to process and journal throughout the week regarding the new information, assisted the couple in identifying the behaviors that enhance their relationship

## A - Assessment

Wally and June appear to have the good will to continue couple's counseling, they are willing to do the assigned homework and are open in session despite their individual pain, both continue to come weekly and there appears to be a strong commitment to working out relationship issues

## P - Prognosis or Plan

Continue working with Wally to decrease his isolation and to re-connect with June when he is in emotional pain, and with June to meet more of her social needs on her own, assigned *Men are from Mars, Women are from Venus* to both in tape form to assist them in increasing their understanding of their different needs and styles of communication, continue to give support and normalize the difficulty of this transition time

So, what did you think? Other than the fact that this therapist gave WAY too much homework and these people are uncannily cooperative with everything the therapist did, the session notes were pretty clear, don't you think? Reading them, you could get a pretty clear picture of what the clients are doing in therapy and where the therapist is going in treatment. Voila! Session notes!

The bottom line is, what you want to do in your session notes is to BE SPECIFIC. Don't let yourself get bogged down in the details of the various disagreements and details of your clients. Remember to think **PROCESS vs. CONTENT.** These are process notes, designed to keep you on track therapeutically and to enable you to provide effective treatment to your clients.

And, if you have a different style of note taking, well then fly, be free. Go for it. This is just ONE example of note taking. If you have one that you've been using that works for you, then don't think to yourself that you need to change it just because a different one is listed in this book. Stick with what works, or even modify what you've been doing to make it work more effectively if need be.

Remember, this whole business thing is about how YOU want to run your business, down to the smallest detail.

One of the truly fantastic resources therapists can now access is the series of book by Arthur Jongsma, Jr. series editor, called *Practice Planners*. For example, you can find *The Adolescent Psychotherapy Treatment Planner* or *The Family Therapy Treatment Planner*. They are simply invaluable for creating and staying on track with therapeutic goals and for tracking the progress of your clients. They can be found in most large bookstores, Barnes and Noble and Borders have them aplenty or you can order them at 1-800-225-5945. On the web, look for www.practiceplanners.wiley.com.

In addition this series also comes in progress note form and are population specific, for example you can find *The Adult*

# Chapter 5    Private Practice

*Psychotherapy Progress Notes Planner*, or *The Adolescent Psychotherapy Progress Notes Planner*. Go to the same place on the Web or access the same phone number for a complete listing.

For note taking, you might also take a peek at TheraScribe, which is a computerized Windows-based clinical record management system. You can get a free demo on-line at www.therascribe.wiley.com.

Other note-taking systems include listing the information under "Data", "Assessment", and "Plan". Under "Data" could be included such things as session goal or overall treatment goals, homework, and current issues. "Assessment" might include reported impairment in daily functioning, assigned homework, and the therapists observations of the effectiveness of the session/treatment. "Plan" could include any assigned homework, prognosis, the goals of the next session, and the scheduled date of the next session.

All session notes should of course include the exact date and the therapists' signature at the end of the session notes. Even if there is additional room on the page, place your signature IMMEDIATELY AFTER the session note and leave the rest of the page blank. This prevents the appearance of impropriety in case your notes are subpoenaed. (If there is room left between the session narrative and the bottom of the page, it looks like you could have "added" to you notes after the fact)

## Crisis information sheet

A crisis information sheet is just what it sounds like. It's an information sheet about what your clients should do in case of a psychological emergency. It should spell out clearly whom the client should call and what your pager availability is (or is not).

If you work on a pager system, then it would include your pager number, and any specifics on how to reach you after hours. Some clinicians include detailed information on their answering machines as to how to reach them in case of an emergency.

But let's say you are one of the mental health practitioners that DO NOT carry a pager. Well then, your information sheet should include phone numbers of whom your clients should call after hours. Perhaps it's their psychiatrist (if they have one), perhaps it's the local crisis hotline number, or it's simply 911. Whatever it is, spell it out clearly for your clients. Have them sign that they got the sheet, give them their own copy to take with them, and place a copy in the client file.

This is a pretty significant legal issue, so be thorough here. You might even want to call your local State or National organization's legal department and have them "proof" it. They'll be able to give you feedback on language and let you know if you are missing anything.

**No harm contract/no suicide contract**

A no harm contract is utilized when you believe that your client is at risk of harmful behaviors. It clearly spells out what the client would do if he/she felt he/she might harm themselves *on purpose or by accident*. I particularly like this phrase because it reminds clients to think "outside of the box." Many people will claim that they are not actively considering suicide, but at the same time they are engaging in extremely high-risk behaviors that could be considered "passively suicidal" or at least dangerous.

A gay man who is engaging in frequent unprotected sex, a teenager who is using drugs and mixing and matching the drugs with alcohol, a woman who is consistently drinking and driving and has gotten 2 recent DUI's: all of these are at-risk behaviors that might not be "officially" considered to be direct suicidal attempts, but which all fall under the category of at-risk behaviors that warrant serious clinical attention. I've found that sometimes languaging this contract as "on purpose or by accident" helps clients dispel the denial that they are "fine" when in fact they are taking unnecessary and possibly dangerous risks with their behavior.

Sometimes clinicians like to put more specifics into their no harm contract. The contract might include a list of names and phone numbers of whom the person will call if/when they get into a bad place. It might include specific behaviors that the client will begin in order to stop the dangerous behaviors. It might even list what the client has to live for. Most contracts include what the person promises to do in relationship to the therapist, for example, "I agree to check in with my therapist every day at 4:30pm."

Many therapists include language of "I agree to", "I deserve to live because", and "I promise to." Of course the client then gets a copy of the contract and you place one in your file.

Be sure to stay up-to-date when you get new information from the client regarding whom he/she may want to contact in case of an emergency, other than you. For example, a boyfriend might initially be listed on the contract, but please **DO** change the contract if/when the client breaks up with said boyfriend. Having the boyfriend's name as a support contact when your client is dealing with the pain/trauma of the break-up is not such a great idea.

## Discharge summary

Another MUST. Be sure to put information about the course of treatment, whether or not therapeutic goals were met, (and why or why not), the reasons for termination or

# Private Practice           Chapter 5

discharge, the condition of your client at the end of therapy, the services provided to your client in the course of therapy, and any additional discharge plans regarding follow-up services needed or referrals recommended.

If the client has left you with no notice, and just decided to "stop" coming to therapy, (and hence there was no official termination session), be sure to also follow-up the termination/discharge session note with a letter to your client. Include in it at least **3 referrals** to other therapists in your area.

Many clients just don't know how to end relationships, therapy or otherwise, and a letter might help them "cap" off their time with you. In addition, sometimes clients just don't know how to say, "This isn't working for me" and so they just leave therapy. (Hence the need for the referrals in order to assist the client is possibly getting his/her needs met elsewhere) Oh, and by the way, the three referral deal is actually an ethical issue, so don't think you're just being a nice guy sending referrals their way. As mental health professionals we are ethically obligated to provide the most appropriate services to our clients, and to give them three referrals if things didn't work out with us. Even if they choose to circle file the letter, you will have done your part ethically.

Need I tell you to keep a copy of the letter in the clients file or does that go without saying? Let's make it easy on ourselves, because I'm sure you're getting tired of hearing me say it. KEEP A COPY OF **EVERYTHING** IN YOUR CLIENT FILE. There, that's done. Now, let's move on.

## Billing sheet (regular)

Keep it simple. A straightforward column style invoice form should do it. Listing the name of the client, date of service, charge, and how much money was collected. You might want to delineate a co-pay column from an insurance column, but others just go with the one column. Your billing sheet should include a running balance amount so that you are able to track your incoming and owed money. This will help you plan financially. It will also help you stay on track with clients who owe you money so that they don't get into a situation where they are drastically behind financially.

*A VERY IMPORTANT note about forms:* there is a great resource if you would like to have all of your form needs already completed and ready for use. It is *The Clinical Documentation Sourcebook*, by Donald E. Wiger. It is a comprehensive collection of ready-to-use blank forms and is specifically designed to assist therapists is managing client records and documenting treatment progress. It also includes handouts, questionnaires, and assessment tools. Again, call 1-800-225-5945 to order or check with your local bookstore.

*A further note about forms:* Wiley also publishes a series called *The Brief Therapy Homework Planner*. Again, it is population specific and if you do brief therapy, it can be a terrific resource for ready-to-use assignments that you can then tailor to the needs of your clients.

## *Affirmations:*

*The forms I utilize assist me in giving excellent treatment to my clients.*

*My documentation for my clients is clear and organized.*

*I am well prepared.*

*I am organized and articulate.*

**NOTES**

# CHAPTER 6: GETTING BUSINESS FOR YOUR BUSINESS

## Advertising

Now I know you want to just skip over this chapter don't you? Advertising and marketing makes MANY therapists nervous, and for a number of reasons. What I hear are things like:

"I don't want to feel like I'm hard selling clients."

"When people are ready to come to me, they will."

"The universe will take care of my referrals."

"Advertising is for *business* people, I'm a *people* person."

"My work speaks for itself."

Fill in a couple of your own. C'mon, own up here. The fact is, unless you happen to be part of the small minority of mental health practitioners who DON'T have a difficult time advertising your services, chances are you have some idea of what it means to market yourself that is interfering with your success as a businessperson. Let's at least get them down on paper so that they lose some of their hold on you. Finish this sentence,

"When I think about marketing and advertising my practice, I . . . "

_____

_____

_____

_____

_____

Let's just put some of this stuff on hold for a minute and take a look at some alternative ways of thinking. People are not going to get to take advantage of your services UNLESS THEY KNOW ABOUT YOU. You can be the greatest people person on the planet and still end up sitting quietly in your office going crazy with boredom unless you get the word out about what you do.

Hard selling is never good for ANY business. And sure, maybe the universe will take care of your referrals, but what about that whole, "G-D helps those who help themselves?" As for tooting your own horn, let's be realistic. For most therapists, this is not really an issue. On the contrary, it usually takes a lot of tooth pulling just to get therapists to talk about what they do, much less brag about it. There are so many confidentiality issues that we must concern ourselves with on a daily basis that, as a group, I believe we have become somewhat reticent to talk AT ALL about who we are and what we do.

The problem develops when John Q. Public hasn't the foggiest idea of what we do because we're so busy not tooting our own horns that we confuse education about therapy with bragging about how we do therapy. Why NOT say, "I'm great with teenagers," or "I do good work with depression and anxiety," or "I can really help those families in transition?" How else will people know?

If you are nervous about this concept, a good transition might be going to one of your local chapter meetings (Like CAMFT) and telling other therapists what you do. Many of us specialize in particular populations or age groups and it's vital to know the resources in our community for referrals for the clients that we may feel less comfortable with.

For example, perhaps you prefer not to see children. That's fine, as long as you ensure that you know of several therapists in my area who DO see children, and whom you would feel happy about making a referral to when the need arises. Perhaps YOUR practice is focused on teenagers; many therapists prefer not working with this age group. Many therapists are desperate to have another professional to refer to when they get a call for one of the 13-18 year old crowd. So it works out. Our clients get what they need from the best person for the job.

But NONE of this is going to happen if you don't get the word out about what you do as a mental health practitioner. So, find a way to get comfortable with it, because if you don't get past this block, it's going to be hard (if not downright impossible) for you to thrive in your practice.

For more detailed information, exercises and practice in this area I would definitely recommend a book called, *Building Your Ideal Private Practice: A Guide for Therapists and Other Healing Professionals* by Lynn Grodzki, publisher W.W. Norton and Company. It is a fantastic resource if you need to focus your time and attention on this area. Ms.

Grodzki takes you through what she considers to be the building blocks of a successful private practice. She helps you articulate your basic message and create, as the title says, your ideal private practice. Ms. Grodzki has a business degree and is a licensed Marriage and Family therapist, and she is able to bring to the table the best of both worlds. So, check it out.

## Newspapers

What a surprise, mental health practitioners are either rampantly <u>FOR</u> or decidedly <u>AGAINST</u> newspaper advertising. Those on the "for" side say it's great copy, lots of people see it, you can reach a maximum number of people with a fairly small output of energy and it's cost effective. Those on the "against" side say that you need to spend too much money for what you get, print advertising of any kind requires an ongoing commitment and repeat copy in order to get the message to "stick" in the mind of the consumer, and it is too fleeting to make a lasting impact.

Are you getting the idea that **THERE IS NO RIGHT OR WRONG WAY TO RUN YOUR BUSINESS**? There are so many ways to set up, maintain, and grow your practice: I am simply trying to ensure that you at least have the information necessary to make an informed choice.

I want you to be armed with enough information to be able to ask good questions.

Be sure to check with the newspaper for their "closing dates" for submission of an ad. Same goes for phone book ads.

## Flyers

Lots of places — supermarkets, coffee houses, community colleges — allow you to put up a flyer advertising your business. There is no cost, very little risk and takes very little time. It can really be one of the easier ways to get the word out. Simply design a flyer with your contact details and then some blurb about what you do and the people you could assist and then post it. (of course be sure to ask permission before you post your flyer)

## MD's/psychiatrists

Much here depends on if you have a personal/professional relationship with an M.D. or Psychiatrist. (When I say personal, I mean a one-on-one personal relationship that is professionally based and grounded, not a we-spend-every-weekend-together personal relationship)

Many mental health professionals have developed strong cooperative relationships with doctors and psychiatrists in their area and they become a referral source for the doctors. A reverse also holds true. If you have found a psychiatrist whose judgment you trust, then he/she becomes a referral source for any of your clients who might benefit from a psychiatric referral.

## Trade magazines (e.g., parenting classes in a parenting magazine)

Don't underestimate the value of placing an ad in a trade magazine. If it is one of the larger magazines, count on taking a pretty decent hit financially for the ad. However, if it is a local magazine (and most cities/counties have a plethora of them), then the cost shouldn't be prohibitive.

In each of the magazines (usually near the front of the magazine and after the list of topics), should be information as to how to contact their advertising department.

## Mailings and professional newsletters

There is a lot of good information available specifically to mental health professionals about mailings of all kinds. Mailings can range from single page fold-overs to newsletters.

You can find good information about this topic through most professional organization newsletters or monthly magazines. Reference books also give you suggestions as to how to format your text, how best to present your information, and how to get direct mailing addresses in your field.

My recommendation is that you invest in a referral book like *How to Create Effective Newsletters* or *How to Build and Market Your Mental Health Practice*, both by Linda Lawless, and published by Wiley.

## Internet/web-sites

More and more therapists are utilizing the Internet for advertising and getting the word out about what they do. At the very least, regardless of how techno-phobic you might be, you can at least have your logistics included in one of the national/state-wide search engines that lists mental health providers by name, license and specialty.

If you are more inclined (and substantially more computer literate), you can develop your own Web site. (And, of course, even if you are NOT more computer literate, this is the perfect time to outsource the job and hire someone to design your website for you)

Therapists who advertise over the Internet have only the best things to say about their experiences. It's basically like having a really really large phone book at your disposal. Keep in mind however, that this kind of advertising will attract a fairly diverse population. (Isn't that saying it in a nice way?) You'll get the full (and I mean full) range of the public at large, so beware.

## Posting at local coffeehouses etc.

An oft-overlooked site for advertising is posting flyers at local restaurants and coffeehouses. Check this out. Who knows who may respond, but it's free, and easy and accessible. Most therapists develop a flyer to post, since a simple business card can so easily get lost in the bigger postings, but it's still a fairly easy way to advertise.

In addition to coffee houses, health food stores, supermarkets, and community centers usually have bulletin boards where you can post your card or flyer.

## Phone books

Don't forget the standards. Phone books, yellow pages, etc allow you to choose from numerous options if you would like to advertise your business there. There are options for the basics, (name rank and serial number), for a business card sized ad, a $1/16^{th}$ page ad, a ¼ page ad, a ½ page ad, and of course, the ever popular full-page ad. (of course, not many therapists new to the profession will choose the latter because you would have to mortgage your firstborn to pay for it, but it's good to know your options)

Prices depend on the phone company and vary greatly, so do some research before you commit. Also, you might want to check with other professionals in your area about their experiences before signing up.

# Referral sources

### Personal

Don't underestimate the potential of getting referrals from people in your personal life; your friend may have an acquaintance, your accountant knows a family in trouble, your pastor thinks a teen might be in trouble. Now, of course, you'll want to stay away from any that might represent possible conflicts of interest, but, other than that, people that know you can be wonderful sources of referrals.

### Other therapists and medical professionals

In the same way that you will have a "Rolodex" system for referring to another therapist, (cf. Chapter 9 on Miscellaneous items including therapist's who specialize), other therapists will gradually get to know your areas of specialty and be able to refer clients to you.

Make sure they know what it is that you do however. Again, if you don't get the word out about what you do, you will not be getting the referrals.

### Giving seminars and/or educational classes

You just can't go wrong with this. Giving seminars and/or classes benefits everyone; you get to sharpen your skills at communication, the people coming to the seminar get to hear expert information, and you may even get some referrals out of it. Now, one obvious drawback is that you have to speak in public. On numerous graded scales, people have ranked only their fear of death as higher than their fear of speaking in public, so this hurtle can be a significant one.

But listen, if you LIKE public speaking, then go for it. If it terrifies you, then skip this as a referral option, and move on to something else more suited to your tastes. If you are on the fence - it doesn't terrify you but you're not thrilled with it either because you are not very confident about your speaking skills - then get yourself to something like Toastmasters or Toastmistress and hone your presentation persona.

Here is a list of possible presentation sites that might benefit from your knowledge:

- Schools
- Professional agencies, counseling or otherwise
- Churches
- Synagogues
- Community colleges
- MFT/LCSW/Psychologist graduate programs
- Training centers
- Internships
- Counseling centers
- "Learning Annex" – classes for the community

## Networking, networking, networking!

A professional I respect once said, upon being asked what pearls of wisdom she would pass on to the next generation of mental health professionals, "networking, networking, networking."

I just can't stress this enough. As you might recall from the beginning of this book (way back when), part of the reason I decided to write this book is that I wanted to begin hooking mental health professionals up with professional contacts and information that only another mental health professional would have. The task of starting a private practice is difficult enough without trying to do it all on your own.

C'mon, we've all been there. Remember getting a new case and throwing every possible intervention at them in the first 4 sessions? Remember all those books you acquired so that you would know what was _really_ going on in that family? There is a great appeal in the neophyte clinician.

But let's not all reinvent the wheel here guys. Qualified people have gone before you, so make use of their information and experience. And therapists, like most established professionals, LOVE to share their information and experiences with the newer members of their "clubs."

Attend a monthly meeting of your local professional chapter. Look for the California Association of Marriage and Family Therapists (CAMFT), American Association of Marriage and Family Therapists (AAMFT), the National Association of Social Workers (NASW), the American Psychological Association (APA) or the National Board for Certified Counselors (NBCC).

Most professional organizations hold local monthly meetings and many put together a yearly conference. Check the WEB for the relevant phone numbers, addresses and upcoming events. Attend them, pass out your cards, note who specializes in areas where you need a referral base and introduce yourself.

Again, you won't get referrals if no one knows what you do, so hang in there, take a deep breath and tell people what you are about.

## Interviewing the masters

Again with the not reinventing the wheel. It is a well-known fact in business circles that one of the best ways to obtain information is to interview someone in your field who is ALREADY SUCCESSFUL and ask them about their business. Ask them how they set it up, how they get referrals, how they managed to stay afloat during the "lean years," how they organize their finances to account for vacation time, retirement accounts and the like. You will glean a wealth of information not to be found in any book or seminar or tape. And you will be able to ask the questions that compel *you*, the questions that keep you up at night. And, last but certainly not least, you will have made a personal connection with someone in your field that you respect and admire.

Now, some fledgling therapists fear by interviewing the masters that they are somehow giving the message that they want to "rip off" the masters. This couldn't be further from the truth.

Already established professionals LIKE to assist the next generation. C'mon, who wouldn't like the questions and shy adoration they would see in the eyes of a disciple? Who wouldn't like someone sitting at their knees waiting with bated breath for whatever pearls of wisdom might drop from their mouths? Everyone likes to be considered successful and most people want to share their successes (and failures) with whoever will listen.

Remember too that therapists and counselors have a somewhat limited audience as far as an understanding of our profession from the general population. I'm sure ALL of us have been at a party and said, "I'm a therapist." People then either fall strangely silent, (mentally evaluating what they have said to you and whether or not it makes them look crazy), or launch into their life story which propels you backwards into the bean dip and guarantees you a wreck of a party because you've just gotten into the clutches of a drunk borderline.

People sometimes just don't know what to do with the fact that you are a mental health practitioner. So how much more thrilling is it to be able to talk to another professional and to glean valuable information from him/her about how to do business?

And remember, no matter how successful that therapist is, you will tailor the information you receive to meet your own needs. I'm certainly not suggesting that you hear what the person has to say and then go make radical changes to your practice that don't fit you. I trust that you will separate the wheat from the chaff and proceed with integrity.

## Getting the word out about what you do

Speaking of which, did I mention that you need to get the word out about what you do? I referenced earlier a fantastic book written by Lynn Grodzki called *Building Your Ideal Private Practice*. In it she describes, in detail, how to set about achieving clarity about what you do and then communicating that to other people. It's really an invaluable resource, especially since it specifically addresses mental health professionals.

Have you ever tried to go to the bookstore and find a business book that could be applicable for therapists? It can be an exercise in futility. But Ms. Grodzki's book is informative, business-based, and practical. I couldn't say enough about it, especially as it relates to getting you clear about what kind of work you do and then letting the world in on your secret.

# Being a provider

### Medi-cal

If you want to become a Medi-cal provider, call first to **your State Capital** and see if there is a contact person in your city or county. Next, call that person. If you get no response, call your county equivalent of Mental Health or Social Services and ask who is in charge of the Medi-cal applications. Most of the time you should be able to pick the application or have them mail you a copy. Complete it, return it and prepare to wait 3-5 weeks for an answer as to whether you were accepted as a provider. In the meantime, familiarize yourself with the wonderful and unique way that Medi-cal does business. It is VERY specific and fairly detail-oriented so might as well get a jump-start on it.

There are different rules for Marriage and Family Therapists who want to see Medi-cal clients. Rather than just doing the initial screening process that everyone has to go through, clients who see Marriage and Family Therapists are also required to go to a physician to justify their need for treatment, so just keep that extra step in mind if this is your license.

### Employee Assistance Programs

Each EAP (Employee Assistance Program) is different so you have to contact each one individually in order to get an application. Employee Assistance Programs work in much the same way as insurance carriers; they approve their members to see one of their panel providers for a certain number of sessions. All paperwork goes to them, and you have to re-submit justification if your client needs more sessions than was originally approved. The EAP pays you directly. As with insurance companies, EAPs may or may not have their clients pay a co-pay. Be sure to check for the standards when you get on the panel.

Despite the fact that EAP's are employment driven and connected, the information is NOT shared with employers or the personnel department. Again, the EAP functions in the same manner as an insurance company. Confidentiality issues remain the same.

Also, clients are "referred" to you by their EAP because you are on their provider panel. This can mean one of two things; either there is a problem or issue with the client and their boss or personnel department has said to the employee, "we'd like you to attend therapy", **OR** the client has approached their personnel department and asked for an EAP referral for whatever personal reason. Don't assume that a referral from an EAP means that your client is having problems at work. The referral method can work either way.

## Victims of crime

Again, you can contact your state licensing agency for information regarding the application process. However, you'll want to contact the District Attorney in your area for an application instead. It doesn't do you any good to apply and have your State Capitol have all your information if you live anywhere *other* than the State Capitol. By going through your local D.A., you'll get on the referral list in your area.

**Private Practice** — Chapter 6

The application process for Victims of Crime is fairly lengthy and includes references and your curriculum vitae, but is definitely worth doing.

You should know though that Victims of Crime recently changed their fee payments from $90/session to $70/session because of the numbers of people currently accessing their funding. And, although Victims of Crime used to have a reputation for long reimbursement waiting times, all the feedback I've received about them in the past several years says that they have straightened out this particular bug-a-boo.

Note: Victims of Crime may be restructuring their referral and treatment process, again because of the numbers of people seeking their services and the concomitant shortage of money that has brought about. They may choose to structure themselves like a traditional insurance company, wherein you are approved a certain number of sessions initially, have to get prior approval for additional, and there is a cap on the total number of sessions allowed. (Prior to this, there was no pre-approval step, no continuing approval and no cap) So, check for any changes in procedure and structuring if you choose to work with this organization.

## Managed care provider panel

You can always become a provider on an insurance panel. I would love to give you an easy, "How To" as to getting on the panel list, but alas, it is easier said than done.

Of course each and every insurance panel is different as to how they would like you to apply and be accepted into their program. Some have a fairly straightforward application process, (lengthy but straightforward). You simply need to call the insurance company and ask for their insurance liaison or insurance representation and ask what you would need to do to become a provider on their mental health insurance panel.

## *Affirmations:*

I benefit my clients.

I market my services with integrity.

I communicate easily and effectively about the services I provide.

I am a good therapist.

I learn from the experiences of others and make the best decisions for my business.

**NOTES**

# CHAPTER 7: MONEY MATTERS

How many clients do you need to cover expenses? How many to make a living? How many do you need to thrive in your business and life? It is VITAL that you come up with a budget.

That being said, everyone has different ways of setting up their budget, and I'm not even going to attempt to suggest one way over another. The point is, whatever your way, DO IT. You cannot simply fly by the seat of your pants with a new business. You really need to have a financial game plan and follow it as closely as you can.

What does your financial budget need to include? Well, at its most basic, business costs and incoming finances. In other words, what's going out each month and what's coming in? Now I know that this can be a particularly fluid thing in the beginning stages of your business. Perhaps more so than most, mental health private practices can be hard to quantify financially when you are first starting out; so much depends on referrals and other sources of income and whether or not you have a "day job" to cover your basic expenses initially.

I'm not saying that you have to have a not-to-be-changed budget, but what you **must** have are the basics, set down on paper, so that you will have an idea of what you have to work with financially. I don't want you to be in a position financially where you don't know WHAT your bills are, much less whether or not you will be able to cover them at the end of the month.

So, come up with a system.

## Money - payment up front or bill insurance and take the co-pay?

Again, there is no right or wrong answer. (I swear to you, there really and truly isn't THE WAY things should be done.) I have heard compelling arguments for both. The fact is, some clinicians can't afford to wait for insurance to pay them, so they bill their clients up front and then bill the insurance afterwards. The insurance company then reimburses the client. Many clinicians, even if they can afford to wait for the insurance money, prefer not to, thinking that a client will be more motivated to follow up on the insurance billing more aggressively if it is *their* money they are waiting for.

Other clinicians will find out from insurance company what the client co-pay is, and then bill the insurance company for the rest of the fee. This can make bookkeeping a bit more challenging, but it seems to be the most prevalent of styles.

(Of course, this all assumes that you are a provider on an insurance panel, or that they have approved you to see their client. It is ALWAYS best to get any and all insurance information at the first session, and then start making calls the next day if you are unsure of the insurance issues.

Unless you are a provider on a particular panel, don't assume that the insurance will cover your services.)

Now, be careful when you get those "big bucks" insurance reimbursement checks. The first few years of private practice can feel so lean that it can be very tempting to splurge when those big insurance checks come in. They can feel like Disney dollars, with little or no immediate connection to all the hours that they represent.

Restrain yourself!!! Return to your budget and sock that money aside for the quieter months. Believe me, there will be quieter months. It is the nature of the beast of mental health private practice that the hours and clients wax and wane. Who among us hasn't heard the axiom about August being a quiet month?

## Quarterly taxes, Social Security and Medicare

One of the lovely things you get to do as a private practitioner is to pay quarterly taxes. You also get the pleasure of paying for ALL of your social security taxes (as opposed to only paying half when you are employed by someone else). And last but certainly not least, you get to kick in for your own Medicare. Yeah! Yippie! Aren't you lucky!!!

So, here are some of the aspects of private practice that are less of a joy than others, so brace yourself.

You'll need to get your self a Tax Identification Number, a.k.a EIN (Employer Identification Number) One of the easiest ways to do this is to go on-line. Check out www.sba.gov. (Small Business Administration) then simply go to the "information needed" area and click on the title for "EIN" (Employee Identification Number).

If you choose, you can do it the old fashioned way, call the IRS or the Social Security Office in your area for a form. You can also check out the IRS Web site at www.irs.gov/business/small.

While you may still be able to use your Social Security Number for tax identification purposes, more and more vendors and banks are requiring that you also have a registered Employee Identification Number. (You MUST have an EIN if you decide to employ people in your business or if you decide to form a Partnership, even if you don't employ anyone outside of the partnership)

Also, having an EIN means that fewer people have access to your Social Security Number: if it is on fewer pieces of paper and in fewer databases there is less chance of anything happening to it. (Your number could get cyber-mugged and end up on the wrong end of a spending spree/identification scam that could cost you time and money and headaches)

(If you're wondering what an EIN is for, it's to help the government track what you're making so that you can be appropriately taxed on that amount. For example, you do some independent contractor work and get paid $1,000.00. By having the EIN, the people you contracted with would then state that they paid you that money. The government then has a tidy paper trail with your EIN number on it to prove it. At the end of the year, they can verify that you represented that $1,000 as income and are getting appropriately taxed on it)

Next, get a form from the Internal Revenue Service, the Social Security office, or Franchise Tax Board in your State to set up your quarterly taxes. If you work for an employer in some other capacity, you might want to have them simply take out additional taxes so that you don't have to pay quarterly taxes on your private practice income. However, most people just do it the "old fashioned way" and file with the IRS or Social Security office in order to set up paying Uncle Sam every 3 months.

# Private Practice — Chapter 7

Be sure to figure Quarterly Taxes into your income base. Many first time private practice people forget to do this and think they are simply rolling in the dough. They forget about Uncle Sam and the fact that they have to pay him now directly. Most of us are used to being employed by someone else who takes our taxes before we even see the money. You don't even think of spending the extra dough because you never really see it to begin with.

Note: you do not need to begin filing your taxes quarterly until you owe Uncle Sam a certain amount of money, and the base number has changed recently, so check with your accountant regarding the circumstances under which you have to begin to pay quarterly taxes.

## Retirement accounts

You probably don't think you have the money to put into a retirement account because you are just starting your business, right? Well, ask yourself, how are you going to have the money "later" when other expenditures might loom on the horizon or you want to expand you business? While it may feel like a "luxury expense," you can't afford NOT to start putting money into a retirement account.

I realize that money is tight, especially for the new private practitioner and it can feel like you just can't afford to be putting money into a retirement account. Later/next year/some other time you'll put in all you need.

But, when you choose to own a private practice business, you are your own employer. There is no safety net, other than the one you create for yourself. That's the joy and the hardship of owning and running your own business. You cannot afford to put this issue off.

Too many people think there is "plenty of time" left before they need to start saving or putting money away for their retirement. There isn't. Remember, once your money is put away, it begins to work for you so that you don't have to work so hard to keep hold of your money.

So, get educated and get committed to putting money into a Roth IRA, a SEP IRA, or a Keogh Plan. A Roth IRA is an Individualized Retirement account and you can max it out every year with a $3,000.00 contribution, which will be raised to $4,000.00 in 2005. (Be sure to keep track of the tax changes so that when that amount is increased, you can take advantage of it)

A SEP IRA is a Simplified Employee Pension Plan if you are self-employed. Currently, (as of 2002) it allows you to put away 13.0435 % of your income or $22,174.00, whichever is less, towards retirement. (note, this percentage and maximum amount changes practically every year, so keep up-to-date on the logistics of the plan)

A Keogh Plan allows you the similar funding of a SEP IRA but gives you greater latitude in the amounts allowed for you to put away. However, the down side is that it is more complicated than a SEP IRA. Check with your bank or financial institution for details.

With all of these plans there are penalties and rules and regulations about the taking out and the putting in of money. Get educated. I personally recommend Suze Orman's, *The 9 Steps to Financial Freedom*. If you still count on your fingers, this is the book for you. It's readable, put in plain simple language, and gives lots of examples. In addition, you can also watch Suze Orman a couple times a week discussing financial issues on a talk-radio type of call-in TV show, or listen to her weekly radio call-in show.

Don't let your finances get out of your control, especially in this regard. Most of us chose mental health work because we are good at it, we like it; we want to make a contribution to the world. However, sometimes those of us with great left side of the brain capabilities are occasionally stunted in our higher math functions. Hang in there.

## Time-off, scheduling it in to your practice

The good news is you're your own boss. The bad news is, you're your own boss. Look, there are some tremendously great things about opening your own business. The whole deal of "answering to no one" obviously appeals to you or you wouldn't have bought this book. Something about this idea really fits your personality.

The not great news though, is that you don't have the "normal" cushion that comes from working in a 9-5 gig in terms of time off and vacation and sick time. Now, normally I would consider this primarily a "Self Care Issue" and so much of my discussion about this topic is headed in the next chapter. However, this is also a money matter.

You want a vacation or want to have vacation time? Then you need to factor that in to your thinking financially. Remember we did the chart on how much money you wanted to make per year? How much would it take to "just get by," how much to do "pretty well" and how much to "thrive"? Well, if you want to have vacation time built into your practice, you have to figure out how much time you want off, and how much money you'll then need to make in order to cover that time off.

Don't make the mistake of figuring out your finances on a monthly basis, rather than on a yearly basis. Otherwise, you'll forget, for example, about August and January, traditionally dead-zones for private practice. These have to be taken into account in your financial planning, especially in regards to vacation.

Much of the same concept applies to sick time. As a therapist, you know that you have to take care of yourself before you can take care of anyone else. Pretty straightforward Therapy 101. But what happens if you are crunched for money? Bills are tight? You had a bad month? It becomes easier and easier in the short term to work when you are sick if you are concerned about putting food on the table. However, you have GOT to factor this one into your "bigger picture."

Forget the lectures, you know the drill. Showing up sick to work in a field such as ours is just plain bad modeling. You want clients to be able to measure their illness and call in sick to work when appropriate? Well, you've got to teach them by example. If YOU show up hacking and coughing, what message could you possibly be sending? Trying to get your clients to work on improving their self-care skills? Not today. You showing up sick to work gives them an automatic "get out of jail free card" to continue to treat themselves with less than the respect that they deserve. So, do everyone a favor and take care of yourself emotionally and physically so that you can also take good care of yourself financially. Give yourself enough of a financial cushion so that, when you *are* sick, you can afford to take off the requisite time needed to get yourself back into fighting form.

I know, I know. Easier said than done. Nothing stresses us out more than needing to take a day off when we have bills piling up and we're just getting started in business. But if you DON'T take that day off, you set up a very bad precedent for yourself that will eventually lead to burnout. So heed my warning, friend.

**Private Practice**                        Chapter 7

## Taxes

My immediate recommendation regarding tax issues is that you get your self educated about the ins and outs of tax law for small businesses. That being said, it is especially important that you keep yourself updated about the laws regarding tax write-offs. If you don't already have an accountant, you might want to get one. While it may seem like a splendid idea to "do your own taxes" and save the money, it is more prudent to hire a professional to manage this side of your business. There have been NUMEROUS tax law changes in the past several years and the last thing you need is an audit, (or the fear of an audit) just because you wanted to save yourself the couple hundred bucks for hiring a tax accountant.

I hate to be a broken record, but again, the learning curve for starting your own business is <u>so</u> steep and there are <u>so</u> many pieces of information that you, as a clinician, need to incorporate into your daily life in the running of a small business that it is simply stupefying. If you are nervous about what you may consider an "unnecessary" expenditure, think of the information you are paying for in having a tax accountant. You will have hired someone who spends all his/her professional hours knowing the most recent tax laws and their applications, leaving you free to pay attention to the running of your business in other areas that might interest you more. However, let me caution you; you still need to know what's going on with your money.

Don't let yourself be so confused by taxes that you just give your accountant a bunch of numbers. Know the laws, (via a book easily obtained at a bookstore on the "basics" of tax law), and then do your homework <u>before</u> you see your accountant. (This way you will also know what receipts to save throughout the year and how to organize your expenditures)

# Chapter 7  Private Practice

So, in general, what are we looking at? There are write-offs that are allowed in every small business, and it would behoove you to know the specifics regarding what you may and what you may not write off. Although I would like to be more detailed about what those allowances are, I am aware that, in the few months that may pass between the completion of this book and its publication, the relevant tax laws might *yet again* have changed. (I'm not kidding, talk to any financial wizard, they'll back me up on this) With that in mind, I want to give you broad categories, not specifics, regarding write-offs.

- You can write off professional materials needed to do your job; books, tapes, supplies, reference manuals. In addition, office equipment and office supplies are also on this list. However, remember that you must be able to prove that these are <u>necessary</u> expenses, and are utilized for your business. You must keep records for your cell phone and computers, in regards to their use in your business, but not for the other kinds of office equipment like copy machines, faxes, calculators (to add up your many riches as a private practitioner!!) and typewriters. Many accountants do recommend though that you keep copies of your the FAX printouts, though, in case there is ever any question about its use.

- You can write off job education expenses. The general rule is you have to be able to prove that the course was necessary for maintaining or improving your job skills. So, conferences, CEU courses, therapeutic intensives (NLP, Narrative Therapy) would qualify.

- You can deduct 50% of meal and entertainment expenses while you are doing job related travel. And that's all I'm going to say about that. The staggeringly large number of specifics involved in these deductions are mind-boggling, and I won't waste your time even trying to explain them to you. Just know they are out there and check out the details in the tax book you undoubtedly will have purchased by now.

- Professional association dues, subscriptions, periodicals are tax deductible as are affiliation dues for organizations like the Rotary Club.

One last note. The IRS expects you to keep a fairly detailed "tax diary" in regards to all of these write-offs. However you choose to do this, be sure you begin it as soon as possible. Trying to recreate the years' worth of write-offs in December can be as pleasant as a root canal (without the numbing drugs) and will likely lead to mistakes that could easily have been avoided by keeping the diary in the first place. If this seems difficult, try filling in your tax diary monthly.

You don't like this need for writing everything down? Feeling frustrated that you have to do it at all? Well, I would love to give you a nice therapeutic re-frame or an alternative way of looking at the situation that might ease your troubled and resentful mind, but here's the deal. This is the way that it is. **GET OVER IT**. The IRS doesn't care about your feelings; they care about your documentation. So find a way to do the deed without losing your mind. You'll save big in the long run and you can sooth your wounded and annoyed self at a spa with all you've saved.

# Billing

### HCFA 1500 form

Gotta love that HCFA 1500, known affectionately as the "Hic-va 1500." This is a form used initially by the medical profession that has made its sweet way into our lives. Many insurance panels have their own billing forms. An equal number used the standardized HCFA 1500. You can order it from the American Medical Association at 1-312-464-5000, or from supply stores found on the Internety. Just type in "HCFA1500" into your browser and you will find suppliers selling 1,000 (a case) for $30.00. You can also occasionally find the forms at one of the larger stationary or office supply stores.

## Billing software

There are lots of billing software programs to fit your business' needs. Quicken is included on most computers or can be purchased at an office supply store.

You can also call the American Medical Association for a CD containing billing software specific to the HCFA 1500, or there are download sites on the Internet. Once the information is input on to the "master file", it will basically fill out your HCFA 1500's as to name, rank and serial number and then all you have to do is put in the applicable billing dates. If you've ever filled out a HCFA 1500, you'll know what a boon this is. They are a royal pain in the you-know-what to fill out: lots of tiny little boxes asking for the exact same information over and over again. (But heaven forbid you should fail to fill out same said information; it will be promptly sent back to you and the process begun anew) Of course this means more time waiting for your money, surely not a good thing regardless of your financial circumstances. So, you might want to check into a specific therapy-billing program. It will save you oodles of time and aggravation.

Note: HCFA 1500 are copyrighted and you are not allowed to make copies of the forms you have. Most insurance companies require that you send in an "original" HCFA

1500, which is printed in red ink. Also, even if you buy the software billing program, you will still have to purchase the red-ink originals.

You can't just print out the HCFA 1500 off of the master file. You will need to load the red ink blank forms into your printer and your file will be calibrated to fill in all the appropriate information. Again, it saves time, but does not let you off the hook from buying the HCFA forms themselves.

## Individual insurance claim forms

Depending on the insurance your client has, you will have to fill out insurance forms. For each provider list you are on, you may have a separate and distinct claim form. They would usually be provided to you by the insurance company and have included in them all of the information that THAT PARTICULAR agency needs to have in order to process the claim.

There are no "standard" forms, unless the company simply requires the HCFA 1500. However, each insurance company with whom you are a panel provider will orient you to their system when they accept you for their panel list. They will send you masters of all of the forms they expect you to complete in your treatment of the case. Be sure to make copies (which IS allowed in this instance). You don't want to have to request additional copies when you discover you've run out. The wheels of insurance companies move <u>extremely</u> slowly and you'll spend weeks and weeks alternately kicking yourself for not making additional copies and burning in effigy the insurance company who has made you jump through such hoops in order to provide some poor soul with much needed help. So, don't let yourself get caught out.

# Chapter 7            Private Practice

## Collecting overdue money

This is not an easy topic to deal with no matter how many years you have been a therapist.

I just don't think there is an easy way to do this, except to say that the more you have set up your policies, the easier it will be to simply refer back to them when overdue money becomes an issue. If you have given you client a written policy list and included on it are your policies regarding collecting overdue money, then you can simply provide your client with a copy of the policy if/when things get behind financially.

Give your clients your policy sheet after you have discussed the issue in therapy: don't just hand them your policy because you are uncomfortable talking about overdue money. Bring in up in therapy, ask them if they had noticed that they were falling behind, ask them what's going on, what they need to get current. Do all of the traditional therapeutic interventions that are appropriate for your clients, and then refer them back to your written business policies.

This can be a GREAT model for therapy and life. Your clients get to see you bring something up to their attention, ask about it, process it, and then problem-solve a solution that works for all involved. What could be better? No shame, no blame, just calm cool problem solving. Perhaps they just need a payment plan to get them started on the balance little by little. Perhaps they could add $10 to each session until they are current. Whatever it is, it CAN be done. Be creative.

Here are a couple scenarios to help keep you on guard against the financial bugaboos. My experience and understanding from other therapists is that usually financial overdue issues develop in the first place when therapists themselves are not yet clear about their policies. I don't care how many pieces of paper you have stating your "policy," if you are uncomfortable or unconscious about your own money issues, then all you've done is simply map out where the bombs are hidden, you haven't actually defused them.

So, try a couple of these on for size.

*A couple comes to see you. He is a successful businessman; she owns a small clothing boutique. They have insurance and are responsible for a $50/week co-pay which he usually pays. They are having relationship trouble and over the course of therapy, decide that they are going to get a divorce. He decides that they should both be chipping in for the co-pay and, to even it out, says he is going to "let" his soon-to-be-ex-wife pay for the next 10 sessions so that they will be "even" and "fair." She doesn't have the money and before you know it, you are $500 behind on co-pays. What do you do?*

*A 19-year-old college student comes to see you. Her parents' insurance has covered her therapy with a minimal $5 co-pay. At the end of the school year her parents dropped her from their insurance in order to "teach her some responsibility." She has stated over and over to you that she thinks she can get her parents to re-instate her on their insurance. In the meantime, the clock is ticking, you haven't been paid and you are starting to feel the slightest twinge of resentment. What do you do?*

*Mother brings her 7-year-old son, Jeremy, to you. Recently her husband was sent to jail and she lost her job. Jeremy has been having difficulty in school and has been suspended twice for beating up other children. The mother states she is has no money and hopes you will be able to see them. She states she is "desperate" for help for their family. You notice that the mother has her nails done every week, and she admits she has "a problem with spending" that she can't get a handle on. She has not paid you for the last two months.*

## Business checking account

You will be able to set up a business account in a couple of ways. If you are a Sole Proprietor, then you will not require a business license in order to set up a business account. You can simply provide them with your name, the appropriate initials after your name and go from there.

However, if you choose to go the route of a tricky fictitious name, you MUST provide the bank with a copy of your business license before they will open a business account for you.

## Business credit card

This one's actually easier to set up than the checking account. Find a card that you like, give them a call. Make sure you list your name, the business name and business address on your application. Even if it's easier to have them send all correspondence to your home, don't be tempted; have it all sent to your office.

Having a credit card specifically for your business will go a long way towards helping you keep track of your business expenses, and taxes will be that much easier at the end of the year.

Watch for the "hidden" and not so hidden costs of credit cards. Check if the card has a yearly fee, late fees (oft times upwards of $35 a pop) or if they're pushing for insurance that costs extra. Also remember, you can ask them to lower your interest rates if you're not happy with the package.

Many companies will be happy to lower your interest rates in order to keep your business.

## Affirmations:

*I have an abundance of money and resources.*

*I navigate and complete financial forms effortlessly.*

*I acquire tax and financial information assiduously.*

*I rely on my own judgment regarding my finances.*

**NOTES**

# CHAPTER 8: SELF CARE

Self-care is one of the most important topics for therapists. We do an incredibly difficult job and without adequate self-care we could just crash and burn, and then do the world no good whatsoever.

That being said, I don't want to waste time preaching to the choir, so let's just dive right in.

## Avoiding therapist burnout

There are probably at least two reasons why therapists leave the field: failure to set up and run their businesses well, and burnout. Burnout is generally a term especially reserved for those in the "helping professions" who have become, to use very official psychological vernacular, "tapped out."

Therapists become burned-out for a number of reasons. Top of the list is self-care (or lack thereof), failure to get adequate professional support, lack of knowledge or skill at setting up their therapy business, and sometimes simply because it's time to move on.

Whatever the reason, this chapter is here so that you are sure that you are CHOOSING to move on, not that you feel so tapped out that you can't imagine doing this job any longer even though you still love it.

So, here are a few suggestions regarding therapist self-care.

## Getting support

There are two kinds of support I am talking about, personal support, (friends, family, religious leaders, acquaintances, etc), and professional support.

First off, here's what I have to say about professional support: **GET IT**. Remember that ours is a very specific and particular field in terms of the psychological stressors. Regardless of your theoretical orientation and your beliefs about the role of the therapist, part of what we "do" is we carry the weight of witnessing the pain of our clients. We have the unique privilege and honor of being a part of an oft-time excruciating process. Sometimes that pain "sticks." We frequently get to see all the parts of the human experience, from the most joyous to the seediest. And, more than anything else, we get to witness the struggle.

Our friends, partners, husbands and wives, bless their souls and regardless of their finest intentions, simply CANNOT understand what this is like for a therapist in the way that another therapist can. So, when I say support, I am talking primarily about professional support.

That being said, I am always amazed (and appalled) at how seldom some therapists get ongoing support from colleagues. Everyone, this is a "MUST DO", don't do this and you are carving the headstone on your profession as a therapist. DO this and you are ensuring yourself years and years of fulfillment, satisfaction, and energy in one of the finest professions on the planet. You think I jest but I couldn't be more serious.

So, find yourself a group, a mentor, or a couple colleagues and meet once a week, once a month, or once a quarter. If you don't know anyone right off hand, check the building you are in. The fact is therapists, like lemmings, tend to congregate. (Well, perhaps little cliff-jumping lemmings are an unfortunate choice of animal comparison. It would probably be better if I went with the traditional "birds of a feather flock together", eh?) Check the building, check with other therapists you know if they have an ongoing group you might join, ask around at a professional Chapter meeting.

And don't worry if you think the group of you might have different ways of doing therapy. Only *some* of the point of getting together professionally is to get professional support. *Another* huge piece of the puzzle is to get Peer Consultation, AKA Peer Supervision. Different theoretical orientations will lead to different points of view on a client, and may help you get "unstuck" when you find yourself at your wit's end with a client.

So jump in. These kinds of groups/meetings can become some of the richest times in your professional day. You get a chance to "talk shop" confidentially, get to hear about the successes and failures of your peers (which is comforting when you are feeling discouraged about some of your cases) and maybe even get to have a little nosh while you're at it. What could be better?

## Affirmations/inspirations

Whatever your belief about affirmations or inspirational saying, if you find them useful in any way then now is DEFINITELY the time to be touting them out.

This could take the form of collages, hand-written saying posted on your bathroom mirror, Hallmark cards tacked to your bulletin board, whatever. It really doesn't matter so long as you are finding solace in the saying. The deal is, this business of starting a business is HARD WORK and can be discouraging at times. So do whatever you need to do to give yourself a little "pick me up" from time to time.

## Anthony Robbins/Dale Carnegie/Dr. Phil

I know this is a bit of a mix of people, but they all have in common the ability to inspire and redirect people towards the achievement of their goals. These are results-oriented people and their materials and tapes can inspire and uplift and move you in the direction of your goals. And if you have a personal favorite whom I have not listed then get their materials. Just do whatever you need to do to get yourself off of the floor if you find yourself facedown on Formica thinking you'll *never* be a good therapist, or you'll *never* have a successful business.

**HANG IN THERE**. It can be done. As the sages say, if ANY man (person) can do it, then **I** can do it.

## Audio tapes/books/movies

Listen to, read things and watch things that inspire you, comfort you, challenge you, and/or relax you. Whatever it is that works for you, DO IT. And don't get stuck in that trap of thinking that you've got to unwind like everyone else. Not everyone is hot wired for the relaxation that comes with yoga, meditation, New Age music, or the latest feel good movie. If it works for you, great, But if it doesn't, then find what does.

Me personally, a nice shoot 'em up bang 'em up movie (preferably one that I've already seen 6 or 7 times) fits the bill to a tee. I get to relax and unwind, there are no surprises in my little video world (because, again, I've seen the thing a half dozen times before and could recite whole passages of the dialogue for you), and I come out the other end of it feeling refreshed and relaxed. When I get done at the end of a therapeutic day/week, the LAST thing I want to hear about, read about, or watch about is some lost soul discovering the meaning of life and getting their life together (or not). I've done my stint with real-life people at that point, and all I want is some cartoon character saving the world, thank you very much.

Now I'm not knocking the people who really do relax in the "traditional" way. But this example is for the people who keep trying to fit themselves into some _idea_ of what it is to relax, and are missing the big picture of how to do it for themselves.

So, here's the deal. EVERYONE DOES IT DIFFERENTLY. Embrace your way and go for it. Whatever it is, if it makes you a more relaxed person, then it's a pretty good thing.

## Journaling

Nothing beats journaling for getting your thoughts and feelings down on paper. (And you thought I was going to say something profound) How many of us, at one time or another, have assigned journaling work to our clients? It's a good outlet, a place to vent, creativity time, whatever. It works to alleviate some of the pressure and anxiety that are sure to come with this new venture of yours.

## Be your best therapist

What would you tell yourself if you came to see you?

What would you say were the things that you needed to do? Breakthrough your fears? Learn self-soothing techniques? Increase your self-care skills?

Every once in awhile it is valuable to stand outside of ourselves and talk to ourselves as if we were our own therapists.

This is particularly important when you need to calm the not-so-encouraging voice that can sometimes arise in the hearts and minds of any new business owner/therapist. I'm talking about the inner voice that bullies you and says things like, "you're not doing enough," "you'll never succeed," "who do you think you're fooling?"

Do for yourself what you would recommend to your clients. Think of what you would tell a person who was starting his or her own business. Think of the "treatment plan" that you would have for that person, how you would tailor it to their particular needs and belief systems. And then, do the same for yourself.

Be your best therapist. Treat yourself with the same gentleness and kindness and comfort that you would show to any client who came through your door that was struggling or discouraged or overwhelmed. Don't just drill sergeant yourself. There is a time and a place for everything and sometimes being a drill sergeant works to get you back on track and motivated and moving. But just as often, you need someone to be kind and gentle with you.

Be your best therapist with yourself. You deserve it.

## Visualizations

If you are not familiar with the basic concepts, just wander into any bookstore and check the categories, "Self-Help" or "New Age." They should have a plethora of information and suggestions on how to get into the whole visualization process and what benefits it will have for you.

## Scheduling in breaks for yourself (including vacations and sick time)

Once you are on your own, you won't get paid time for vacations and sick time and "mental health days." There is no longer anyone who is going to give you "credit" for the time you have worked and have that "credit" be applied to time off. You have to do all of that yourself. No more county organization or counseling center giving you Columbus Day off and Labor Day off and paying you to boot.

So you've really got to schedule that into your calendar. It may not seem like such a big deal in the beginning when enthusiasm runs high and you are taking any business that comes your way. But after awhile, (and not that long of a while), you will begin to be very tired. You will need a break. So, schedule breaks in for yourself. (And that includes vacations, sick time and "mental health days")

Assume that you will not always feel your most empathic, most supportive, or most listening self that you would want to be. That's because you are TIRED. So don't ignore it. It can be tempting when you are first starting out, when bills seem higher than income and you are not sure of your overall money levels. But don't let the temptation of the short term "push" get in the way of legitimate R & R.

Our profession has an extraordinarily high burnout rate. We help people, we listen to them, and we "hold" their pain for them until they are ready and able to hold it for themselves. But we cannot be like the proverbial cobbler whose children are barefoot. We MUST care for ourselves or we will have nothing to offer those who come to us for care.

We've all given the same "suggestion" to the overworked mother who is trying to be all things to all people, to the frenetic businessman running, running to make yet another sale, to the college student who doesn't balance study time with play time.

Schedule yourself some R & R. It's not a luxury, it's survival. You don't want to be one of those "pinched around the eyes" stressed out therapists who looks like they haven't taken time off in years and is simultaneously trying to convince their clients that "Self-Care" is important while they are not-so-slowly circling the drain. Don't be the cobbler. It's what you would tell your clients to do, so take a wee bit of your own advice and take care of yourself personally so that you will be WELL professionally.

Plan for the same kind of "vacation package" in your private practice that you would get in most organizations, namely one day/month vacation time and one day/month sick time. Over the course of a year, that means planning to make 24 more days worth of money to cover for what you would be "taking off." It may mean only adding one hour a week to your current schedule; one hour/week times 52 weeks @ $50.00/session equals $2,600.00. That may be enough to cover for your days you are setting aside for vacations and sick time. If not, figure out what you WOULD need and put it down on paper. (Also, don't forget to ask yourself, does your rent increase each year? Do you increase your fees to cover additional costs over time? Factor these in to your time-off equation.)

And don't forget about the smaller breaks. An hour or two off here and there can go a long way towards making you feel refreshed and ready for your next client. Take a walk, go to lunch, or go hang out at the Mall. But whatever it is, make sure it is actually RESTFUL to you. If the Mall stresses you out because you can't buy anything at the present due to your "austerity budget", then go somewhere else, and for heavens sake, don't white-knuckle it if you don't have to.

## Exercise

You've got to love something that can actually be all things to all people. (Or at least many things to many people) Feeling a little down? Exercise will help lift your spirits. Finding yourself a tad anxious? A nice heart-rate increasing activity is just the thing to settle you back down on the planet.

So, find yourself a nice activity that makes you smile and go for it. This particular form of self-care will take you a long way towards feeling calm and confident about your future prospects in the filed.

And there are NUMEROUS books and classes and tapes you can utilize in your exercise vision quest. Regardless of how much time you do or don't have, there is sure to be an exercise program that just perfectly fits the bill for you.

## Your own therapy/support group

A MUST. You have GOT to have some form of a support system professionally, and I mean an emotional support system, not just a professional network or lunch buddies and colleagues. The best-case scenario would be to have a "group" (therapy or otherwise) or an individual therapist. I'm sure then, when countertransference rears its ugly head, you'll be in an already established relationship and can process your stuff at will. Otherwise, when the crucial time arises, you'll be stuck scrambling to get the support and insight you need to get through whatever it is that you're going through.

## Taking professional enhancement seminars/continuing education

Most of our professional licensure organizations require some form of continuing education credits each renewal period, and there's simply no reason that some of these can't also fulfill personal needs we might have regarding certain topics.

Take courses that interest you. This will make you feel better about, Number 1, spending the money, Number 2, spending the time away from the office (and therefore not making any money) and Number 3, spending time on something that you're not convinced you could do without.

Whatever you do, don't take courses that make you ask, "Why would someone ever WANT to take this class?" Of course, most of the reasons that people say the above listed foolish thing is because they have waited until the last minute to gather together their 36 (or whatever) hours of continuing education credits and their license is due to expire in 12 hours.

A word to the wise. Start early. Those 2 years can pass quickly, and even though most licensing organizations merely audit files randomly, you really don't need the angst of wondering if you're going to be one of the lucky few listed in your professional magazine under "disciplinary actions."

I know I've mentioned this before but be sure to find out what SPECIFIC requirements your licensing organization has regarding these continuing education credits. Do you have to take a Legal and Ethical course every 2 years? Perhaps update your HIV information? What about drug and alcohol courses? Whatever it is, be up-to-date on it. It will save you time and money in the long run.

## Going on retreat

Participating in a personal or professional retreat can make an enormous difference to your peace of mind and mental well-being. Although the cost may seem prohibitive, they are worth it. Just think about it, two or three days sans the kids, partners, phones, paperwork, and pets. Rest and relaxation, maybe a couple good seminars, maybe just a few good walks. Whatever the set-up, it will help ensure that you don't crash and burn in this sometimes crazy business of ours.

## Massages/facials/the pampering world

Need I say more? Who actually needs convincing that getting a nice massage or facial would be a fantastic thing? I personally recommend *at least* once a month for a start and more frequently once your practice starts to be more demanding.

And don't worry so much about the finances on this one. If you are concerned $$-wise (and who isn't who when starting a new business?) then check out any of the massage or beauty schools in your area. They have terrific prices because their students have to "log in" a certain number of hours. And you get an enthusiastic, eager student who has hot-off-the-presses information about the latest and greatest techniques. A Win-Win all 'round.

## *Affirmations:*

*I care for myself.*

*I schedule in time away from the office in order to meet my own needs.*

*I am loving towards my body and care for its needs.*

*I am fit and full of vitality. My physical strength enables me to meet my business goals.*

**NOTES**

# CHAPTER 9: MISCELLANEOUS

## Sole proprietorship vs. partnership vs. incorporated

Sole proprietorship pretty much means exactly what it says. You own the business, you run the business, and you ARE the business. This means legally as well as logistically. Basically, the deal is, you are the beginning, middle, and end of your private practice. Someone has a problem? They come to you. On the opposite end of the spectrum, someone has a compliment? Again they will be coming to you.

The good news is: you have complete Napoleonic control over every little detail of how your business gets run, from the office décor to the stationary to the kind of tissues you want your client's to pamper their little noses with. The bad news is: *you've got complete control over every little detail of how your business gets run.* Either way you look at it, it still stands at: the business is yours.

Partnership is also pretty much what it sounds like. You and one or two of your friends/colleagues decide to get together and run a joint business. You can both be mental health practitioners, but it's not necessary that you have the same degree or license. You also have the option to decide about the division of labor, as it were, and to put down on paper what will be each of your responsibilities to the business. That means you don't have to share everything 50/50. If one wants/is able to front more on the money side you just need to make that clear in your "charter."

The key issue here is BE CLEAR. It doesn't matter how you choose to set up your partnership, what matters more is how you communicate so that things are clear between the two of you. How much money will each put into the business? How will profits be split? What about responsibilities regarding business accounting and billing, who takes care of what? How will you handle disagreements?

An attorney is a good idea once you have the basics ironed out. Check on the logistics and legalities of what you've come up with. Many of you reading this will be going for Sole Proprietorship, but it's good that you at least have the information about your options. Perhaps down the road you may choose to do a Partnership, at least now you've been introduced to the basic issues.

Also, know that there are lots of computer programs available that would allow you to put together the basics of a Partnership or Incorporation *before* you go see an attorney. This will save you lots of money in the long run.

And finally, I think it's a good idea for you to know about incorporation. I won't even <u>attempt</u> to go into the details of incorporation with you because I'm assuming that most of you reading this are shooting for simply getting started in your first private practice venture, but I want you to know that incorporation is a possible option for you professionally, perhaps further down the road.

Incorporation is a fairly technical legal standing that could mean you are doing business alone, and it could mean that you are doing business with others.

Incorporation is not for the faint-hearted and I just don't want to scare you with the details of how to go about getting incorporated. Suffice it to say that Incorporation can mean being more protected <u>personally</u> from legal action taken against your business, but it entails TONS more paperwork and logistics in order to set it up.

## Fictitious business names, a.k.a., "doing business as" statement

Step #1

Easy form to fill out on this one. You have to go to your local county government agency, either the courthouse or the county clerks office and ask for a form to file for a "Fictitious Business Name." It only costs about $30 and it allows you to do business under, you guessed it, a fictitious name. If you choose to have your name be your business name, Angela Mohan, MFT, then you do NOT need to file for a fictitious business name. But anything else, you do.

Now, filing for a fictitious business name doesn't mean that you can't still be a sole proprietorship business. You can still be the one and only in your business and have a fictitious business name. "Creative Counseling Services" might be what you're in love with and you could be the only therapist in the service. That's fine, just be sure to file for the name.

What the filing also allows you to do is to lock in your business name for the next 5 years. (At the same time, you may find upon filing that someone has already taken up your beloved "Creative Counseling Services" in which case it's back to square one with the name issue) Keep in mind that you have to renew your name every 5 years.

## Step #2

Once you've filed for your fictitious business name, you'll need to publish a public notice that basically tells people what your business name is. Check when you turn in your form to the clerk's office as to whether or not the newspaper gets notified when you file your fictitious business name, or whether you'll need to notify the paper yourself.

## Step #3

Provide verification to the clerk's office that you did the publication stuff. While the newspaper might do this for you automatically, double check on the chain of information so that you don't miss anything (e.g., if you don't give the verification, your business name could become invalidated, so stay on top of things).

## Step #4

Put a copy of your business license in a file in your already set-up filing cabinet and make a note to yourself to do the same all over again in 5 years.

## Referring to a medical professional

One of the first things you will need to do once you've established where your practice will be located is to find a good psychiatrist with whom you feel comfortable working. Same goes for a medical doctor, an internist and a gynecologist. You need to have a solid referral base of professionals whose work and opinion you trust. Remember that 45-year-old woman you suspected of having hormonal issues? Well, you need to be able to give her the name and number of a professional you trust. She may have her own OB/GYN but if she doesn't, you'll feel more comfortable making a referral to a professional you know.

This may mean getting out there and meeting some of your neighbors and letting them know you are in the area. Drop off a few cards. Call a psychiatrist up and introduce yourself. Tell her/him you are looking for a possible referral base and wanted to spend a few minutes with her/him over the phone. Talk about the services you offer. Ask about the services they offer. It may end up being mutually beneficial.

Talk to other therapists in the area and find out whom they like. As you get to know your "neighbors," you'll start to develop contacts with other therapists and mental health providers. Ask around at your local chapter meeting. Talk to your colleagues about who is good to work with, who never returns calls, who "plays well with others."

In addition to psychiatric and medicals referrals, you should probably also have on hand referrals for a pediatrician, mediator, attorney, (of various kinds), accountant, business coach, low or no fee therapy clinics, group therapy center, and issue-specific groups. (Cancer support group, adolescent anger management group, etc)

## Referring to another mental health professional

And let's not forget referring out to another mental health professional. Shall I return to the theme of, "don't try to be all things to all people?" No matter how fantastic you are as a therapist, there are going to be kinds of clients that just don't float your boat. For me, it's the under-fives. Enough with the play toys and the sand and the *stuff* everywhere; it's just not my cup of tea. I see lots of families, (and I LOVE working with teenagers) but the little ones I prefer to send on their merry little Dr. Seuss way. That means that I have to have pretty solid referrals for other mental health professionals in my area.

Now, I'm not saying that each of us couldn't see these people in our own offices, nor am I saying that you need to specialize in every single one of these areas in order to be qualified to treat these clients. The fact is we all have the education, training and experience to provide treatment to any of these client populations. But having the *ability* to provide treatment doesn't mean you have the *desire* to provide treatment.

There will always be clients we want to refer out, maybe because our practice is so busy, maybe because we have 15 of that kind of client already and need some diversity, maybe because we just want them to see someone who only specializes in that area. It doesn't matter what the reason, just know that you need to have your ducks in a row and know the referral sources in your area.

My recommendation is that you familiarize yourself with the professionals in your area who specialize in the areas of practice that you don't. For example, develop a list of referrals for:

- Art therapy
- Grief work
- Trauma
- Adults Molested as Children
- Anger management men's group
- Teenagers
- Cancer survivors
- Divorce
- Step-parenting
- The list could go on and on

This process may be a fairly lengthy one. Don't worry about that piece of the process. Don't just look in the phone book and pick out a bunch of referrals that fit particular areas. These should be really good sources of information for you and they reflect upon your professionalism, so take your time to develop this list.

## Insurance issues

<u>Business Insurance</u> is a must. This is the insurance that covers you and the people who come in and out of your office for things like "slip and falls", etc.

Also on the business insurance side of things are insurance for fire, vandalism, theft. You'll probably be able to get a decent package. Call around. Some buildings require proof of business insurance; some buildings may already have insurance for the building that covers your particular office, so check before you buy.

<u>Malpractice insurance</u> is also high on the list of first things to do. Chances are, you have already been set up and covered as an intern, so either go with the same company, or check with your State or local professional agency for their recommendations. Most Malpractice insurance allows you to amortize based on the number of hours you work, part-time, full-time etc.

<u>Health insurance</u>

Well, what is there to say about this? Do whatever you can to cover yourself medically. I know it may seem like a burden, but all it takes is one accident, one medical snafu to put you in the hole financially. Don't let yourself think that you can do without health insurance. Yes the monthly premiums may seem high, especially when you are trying to keep yourself to a strict budget, but it's necessary.

## Chapter 9 — Private Practice

<u>Disability insurance</u>

The camps are divided on this one. Me personally I'm a big believer in disability insurance, especially since I'm the one and only person in my business, and if anything happens to me I'm out, well, my entire income. I think disability is also especially vital when you consider that, as therapists, most of us will be working for ourselves or in a partnership. Again, without our labor, there's no money coming in.

There's no County plan or Clinic sick time or vacation time to rely on to cushion an emergency. And how many of us (really) have the recommended 8 months of savings tucked away? (Oh, and by the way, that 8 months time frame isn't just something I made up for effect. That's actually a fairly standard recommendation by people "in the know" in the financial world. Yup, they say each and every one of us should, at each and every point in our professional lives, have 8 months worth of whatever we would need financially in order to keep our lives afloat. Staggering, isn't it?)

So, look into this. The premiums aren't so bad, and it can (literally) pay off in the long run. Think of it this way; let's say you were laid up for 5 months for whatever reason. You then at least have SOMETHING coming in. (assuming of course, that *somehow* you were one of the FEW of us who didn't have their requisite 8 months in the mattress)

And the issue becomes more important if you have little ones to provide for. So, enough said. You get the picture. Do it. Bite the bullet and just do it.

Note: As a self-employed person you may be able to purchase state disability insurance from your state.

## Legal issues/legal consultation

We all hope this will never be an issue, but we need to be prepared for all possibilities.

Most mental health organizations offer their members legal consultation *pro bono*. You can simply call them up, give them your membership number and ask them your relevant legal question.

In addition, many organizations recommend, (and in some cases require) you to attend a Legal and Ethical Seminar once every 2 years. If you're ever tempted to complain about this requirement, don't. Many therapists have had some tricky legal question answered at these seminars, and these answers have subsequently saved their professional careers, so hang in there and know they will be worthwhile. Besides, they're usually pretty interesting, despite the normal "dry-ness" of legal issues.

## Licensing issues

Each of the mental health professional groups has specific licensing requirements. I am not even going to *attempt* to go into them at this stage of the game. Number one, you probably know them better than I. Number two, you are probably already licensed, (or about to be), hence your interest in this book. Third, the licensing issues can change and heaven forbid I give you information that ends up being obsolete over the course of the next few months and you waste your time following old information. I trust that you know what you need to do in order to get licensed.

That being said, I would like to remind you to stay on top of your licensing requirements. This could mean continuing education credits, license renewals, alerting your relevant licensing organization of an office address change, whatever.

# Chapter 9 — Private Practice

The point is, don't get yourself in a jam over a technicality that is easy to handle ahead of time.

Your licensing board has no problem holding up your license renewal over a "technical" issue like not having your correct address.

## City business license

You will need a State license in order to practice in your city. In addition, you need a city license to do business in whatever city you are doing business in. You need a city license so that the city can tax you for the pleasure of doing business in their fair area. Call your County Clerk's office to find out where you need to go in your city. Sometimes the city offices are housed in County courthouses or county Offices, and sometimes they are in their own section of government offices, but not county affiliated. A couple phone calls are all you should need to figure this one out.

Parlay alert: this may be the same office where you would need to file your fictitious business name, so check that out. It may save you a trip later.

## Continuing education

Licensed Marriage and Family Therapists, Licensed Clinical Social Workers, Licensed Professional Counselors, and Licensed Psychologists now all have continuing education requirements built into their license renewals.

Be sure to keep up-to-date on the particular requirements of your license. Pay particular attention to specific classes that your specific licensing board may want you to take. For example, California Marriage and Family Therapists are required to take 36 hours of continuing education within each 2-year period, but the California licensing regulatory board has added a particular Law and Ethics class it requires Marriage and Family Therapist to take. This is a "must-do" and will ultimately account for 7 units of the continuing education credits.

With a few exceptions like this one, your licensing board will let you all take whatever you'd like for continuing education, so pick the courses that interest you the most and that are given by an approved provider. Some people choose to take a "program intensive" that runs for several days. Others choose to take discreet one-day classes on a variety of topics. It's wholly up to you. Keep an eye on the "big picture" though, when you choose your classes. Ask yourself; does this class propel me forward in the goals and vision of my practice?

Be sure to keep your certificate verifications, preferably in a separate file folder in your office cabinet. Do NOT send them to whomever tracks your continuing education credits. They are for audit purposes only. Also, if you have some reason you have <u>not</u> completed your continuing education credits within the prescribed time period, know that your license goes on hold until you fulfill the credits. This could mean lots of money lost to you, so keep on top of this. If there is a good reason for you're not having done the classes, log on to the relevant consumer licensing website and find out their waiver procedures.

## Diagnostic and Statistical Manual of

## Mental Disorders

You've really got to have one, like it or not. You may subscribe to any belief you'd like about pathology, but you <u>must</u> follow the guidelines set forth in this charming little tome in order to diagnose and treat your clients. In addition, you've got to know this stuff for insurance billing, case management, treatment planning etc. They're not too terribly expensive when you consider how much you'll use them and how long they'll last, but they can be a bit of a breath-taker when you've got to shell out $50-$100 (depending on paperback, hardback and Textbook Revisions) for one just when you're starting out and feeling broke.

You can get the current DSM IV or the DSM IV-TR, which has Textbook Revisions in it. The Textbook Revision edition is slightly more expensive but also more up-to-date.

If you are feeling like you could use some diagnostic brush-ups, you can also get a DSM IV Casebook, which has loads and loads of diagnostic vignettes and "real life" client scenarios to assist you with differential diagnosis and assessment issues.

## Code procedure book (CPT)

Much less necessary for your practice, but you must at least have access to one. This book includes all the codes for treatment of your clients. For example, it will give you the necessary codes for a 50-minute psychotherapy session. Most therapists do not choose to buy a CPT codebook however, because they generally utilize only a few codes; 50 minute, 23-30 minute, family session etc. If you can get hold of a CPT codebook and write down the codes you need then you'll save yourself a bundle. You can also find CPT information on the Internet.

## Business files

Make a decision as to how you want to set up your filing system. Many therapists go for the straight and easy filing system of last names then first names filed alphabetically.

A growing number are now filing according to "topic". For example, they might file their clients under last names and then file the rest of their business documents under topics such as "utilities", "insurance purveyors", "continuing education" etc. There is no right or wrong way to organize your business files. Whatever works for you is the key. Your files should be organized in such a way as to make sense to you. It doesn't matter how you file, so long as it makes sense to you and you can easily access the information you need as you go through your day.

Listed are some of the types of file headings that I recommend as a guideline for your beginning file system.

- Clients
- Contracts
- Utilities
- Memberships
- Continuing education
- Seminar brochures
- Expenses
- Professional contacts
- Business license/fictitious business name
- Therapists' who specialize in particular areas. This is the "rolodex" equivalent of a filing system. Put any flyers, advertisements etc in this file.

So, that's it for now everyone. Thank you for giving me this opportunity to share my knowledge and experiences with you. I certainly hope that this guide has proved to be useful to you in getting started on your small business ventures.

Good luck to you in the exciting months and years ahead. Know that you're on the right track and trust that you are doing what works best for you in your practice. Hang in there and be good to yourself.

## *Affirmations:*

*I incorporate new information easily and effectively.*

*My business decisions accurately reflect my values and beliefs.*

*Yes, I can.*

*I am able to access information with ease, and incorporate that information into my practice in a way that best suits my professional values.*

**NOTES**